WHEN A PRINCESS DIES

Harvest Books has been created to extend
the *Harvest* journal by publishing in book form
studies which cannot be contained in journal form.
Continuing the non-sectarian tradition of the journal,
Harvest Books aims to publish works from
the wide spectrum of Jungian psychology.
This book is the first of the series.

When a Princess Dies

Reflections from Jungian Analysts

Edited by

JANE HAYNES and ANN SHEARER

HARVEST BOOKS

Harvest Books

Series Editor: *Renos Papadopoulos*

Published by the
C. G. Jung Analytical Psychology Club, London
P.O. Box 19017, London N7 6WQ
Registered Charity Number: 299736

First published 1998

ISBN 0 95 336790 8

Typeset by Regent Typesetting, London
Printed and bound by The Cromwell Press
Trowbridge, Wiltshire

Contents

Acknowledgements

The publication of this book owes a great deal to the support of the C. G. Jung Analytical Psychology Club, London and Renos Papadopoulos. Early drafts of our own articles appeared in *SAPLINK*, the Newsletter of the Society for Analytical Psychology (No. 19, October 1997; No. 21, July 1998). Our typesetter John Smith tolerated our ignorance with an unfailing patience, Roulla Papanicolaou read the text for us and Iris Walker organised distribution. Our thanks to all concerned, especially to the contributors who worked so hard and with such good heart.

The quotation from 'Sailing to Byzantium' on p. 89 is reproduced by kind permission of A. P. Watt Ltd on behalf of Michael B. Yeats.

Jane Haynes and Ann Shearer

Introduction

JANE HAYNES AND ANN SHEARER

The death of Diana, Princess of Wales, after a car crash early on 31 August 1997, led to an unprecedented outpouring of public emotion, not just in Britain but across the world. A year later, we are still trying to understand what it was about her that drew such a response and what that response might say about the times in which we live. This collection of essays by Jungian analysts, all of whom work in Britain, is part of that attempt at understanding.

Why should analysts want to enter a field so well worked by social and political commentators? At its simplest, we probably have more than our share of the human urge to understand other people and what they get up to. But more than that, we know from experience that life very often *is* stranger than fiction, and perhaps our orientation allows us to tolerate strangeness, rather than explain it away. Jungian analysts also draw on theoretical concepts which seem to have particular relevance. Individual Jungians have very different emphases and personal approaches, especially evident when, as here, they are writing not theoretically but subjectively, not from their heads but, as it were, from their middles. But still, we would probably all take as building blocks Jung's concept of the collective unconscious that underlies the personal; his idea that there is a compensatory relationship between unconscious and conscious attitudes; and that the symbolic image mediates the archetypal world to consciousness. We can wonder, for instance, what it was that exploded out of the collective unconscious with Diana's death, and what it was that made the figure of the dead princess, who moved so constantly between high and low, such a powerful mediator between the conscious and unconscious realms. The questions transcend national and cultural boundaries, as archetypal questions always will.

In asking such questions, we are not seeking to turn Diana into 'a case history'. We are not interested in the analysis of a corpse, nor do we wish to anatomise fragments of her psyche. Our questions, which are as much about the mysteries of ourselves, do not seek to expose her enigma. Yet as these essays show, the distinction is not always easy to maintain. Diana disclosed so much of her privacy in public that she almost gave people permission to become bodysnatchers; she invited us to become 'experts' about her. At the same time, the blurring of boundaries between collective and personal, which was so much part of her power as mediator, can also make it hard to know whether we are talking about 'her' or 'us'.

For many of the people who surged across London in their thousands in that first week of September to lay their flowers, or queued for hours to sign the books of condolence, that often seemed the most important thing of all. 'You felt you knew her', they said, over and over again, each cherishing the idea and image of their own Diana, their own lost princess. Did we know on that first morning, as the broadcasting media began its own week long vigil between death and funeral, just how much psychic energy she carried for so many? One of us remembers, on that Sunday, sitting on the London Underground opposite a pale and sad young woman who was clutching a small bunch of flowers. It was hot, she was clearly uncomfortable in a black woollen suit. She evoked passing sympathy: it was probably her only black; she was on the way, perhaps, to a family ceremony; a recent bereavement, someone close? Even when she anxiously asked which was the nearest station to Kensington Palace, the penny didn't drop.

By the next morning, a huge body of feeling had already emerged from that one small remembered cell. Later, critics were to claim that the manifestation of public emotion had been media-made. But to begin with at least, the media followed something that was already organically growing. Each of us will have our own selective memories of that week which culminated in the funeral, when Saturday became Sunday and Sunday became secular by comparison with Diana's day. But like the days of that week, memories become blurred. So here, to set a context, is a reminder of some events and images.

Diana, Princess of Wales and her lover Dodi Fayed crashed just after midnight in a motor tunnel in Paris, when their speeding car, chased by *paparazzi*, smashed into a pillar. He and the driver were killed outright. She was taken to the Pitié Salpêtrière hospital, where by 4 am she was pronounced dead. Later that day, the Prince of Wales, on holiday with his children and their grandmother in Balmoral, flew to Paris, together with Diana's sisters, to accompany her body back to London before returning immediately to his children in Scotland.

Tony Blair, the Prime Minister, had already coined the phrase which was to define both Diana and the spirit of the week to come. 'She was', he said, 'the People's Princess and that is how she will stay, how she will remain in our hearts and our memories for ever'. By the end of that first day, the Princess's people had already gathered in their thousands at Buckingham and Kensington Palaces to leave their flowers, notes, and trinkets. As the week went on and the crowds grew, only aerial photos could encompass the scale of it. Where is the vocabulary to convey the atmosphere of such a public manifestation? The statistics can persuade us of its importance by telling us it was big and by the end of it all there were statistics galore. An estimated 600,000 people signed the books of condolence at Kensington Palace, another 130,000 at St James's. By mid-week, Buckingham Palace had received 100,000 messages on its website and, by mid-September, 500,000 letters and 580,000 e-mails. In those first nine days, the gates of the palaces were wrapped in 10,000 tons of flowers – an estimated 50 million blooms – and another 150,000 tons of tributes ranging from champagne to teddy bears. Fifty people reported seeing visions of the princess around Kensington Palace. Churches ran out of candles.

None of this, of course, says anything about the mood of those days, or of the people behind the statistics. Paradoxically, it seemed a week of extraordinary calm. They say the crime-rate went down. High Street shops reported a £250m drop in trade. On one visit at least,the people pushing their flower-bearing toddlers towards Kensington Palace didn't grumble through the crowds but smiled at each other in recognition of a shared journey . A late night visit to St James's found many still there, and again this sense of reflection, of purpose shared even with the police, whose sterner face was so evidently not needed. It was all very quiet . You could hear a feeling of unity.

Unity? Diana lost her royal title after she and the Prince of Wales divorced. As this week showed, and as her brother Earl Spencer was provocatively to underline in his funeral oration, she had no need at all of it to 'generate her particular brand of magic'. But if Diana did not need the Royal Family, it increasingly seemed that they, and the very institution of the monarchy, needed her.

Where did Diana belong? When her body returned from Paris, the coffin was draped in the Royal Standard; but there was no ceremony when it arrived in Britain and it was taken to a private mortuary before being transferred to the Chapel Royal at St James's Palace the next morning, The Palace confirmed that the Princess would not have an official state funeral, but rather 'a unique service for a unique person'. But as the week went on, the proposed ceremony acquired more and more of the panoply of state. The coffin would be borne to Westminster Abbey by a gun carriage of the King's Troop, Royal Horse Artillery – a dignity accorded only six times in this century, for three monarchs, Churchill, the Duke of Windsor and Lord Mountbatten. The funeral route, we learned, would be extended to start from Kensington Palace, rather than St James's as originally planned.

Yet how 'public' and how 'private' was this funeral to be? In life, Diana had seemed torn between her public and private faces; the issue still seemed to pursue her. When her death was announced, the politicians stopped their campaigning on Scottish and Welsh devolution and the Football Association cancelled all the day's matches – something it had last done in more deferential times, after the death of George VI. On the day their mother died, her sons went as usual to Crathie church, with their father, grandmother and family, and not a word about the tragedy was mentioned. Criticism of the Royal Family's decision to remain at Balmoral grew, in the popular prints at least. This, it seemed, was not an occasion for the accustomed privacy of grief. 'Show Us You Care', *The Express* urged the Queen. 'Where is Our Queen Where Is Her Flag?' demanded *The Sun*. And was it Diana's 'people' or the Queen's who so petitioned? *The Mirror* declared its loyalty: 'Your People Are Suffering – Speak To Us Ma'am'.

We seemed to need a show of unity to heal the much-publicised bitterness between Palace and Diana: the Princess's people wanted to be the Queen's as well. The demand that the Monarch show she shared – approved of? understood? forgave? – the public mood focused on three gestures: the public presence of the royal family in London, a television broadcast by the Queen and a flag at half mast on Buckingham Palace. Such is the strength of symbolic gesture that the first two seemed the more easily achieved. Whatever the private cost. The Queen and her family returned from Balmoral not on the day of the funeral as planned, but the day before. They walked about in public to show appreciation of the tributes and the crowds. The Queen, in a live television broadcast, united the public and private realms when she said that she spoke 'as your Queen and as a grandmother'; she paid her own tribute to Diana as an 'exceptional and gifted human being', who made many, many people happy.

The question of the flag carried far more of the essential issue. The Queen, unprecedentedly, had ordered all flags on public buildings to fly at half mast at the beginning of the week – something that many were doing anyway. But the Royal Standard still flew at full-mast at Balmoral while she was there and no flag at all had flown over Buckingham Palace. This, we were told, is the way the presence and continuity of the monarchy is symbolically signalled. Only the Royal Standard is flown over royal palaces, and then only when the Monarch is present. It is never flown at half-mast because the moment of death of the reigning monarch is also the very moment of the successor's accession. But 'the people' demanded a different symbolic message, and they got it. For the first time ever, the Union Flag was flown from Buckingham Palace, and at half-mast too, from the time the Queen left for the funeral until midnight. 'It is', said the Palace, just as they had of the funeral plans, 'a unique occasion for a unique person'. In her life, and in her death, Diana broke the bounds of tradition. In her death she also, symbolically and briefly, broke the continuity of the British monarchy.

Yet she went to her funeral wrapped in its protection, her coffin still covered by the Royal Standard. On her lonely procession from Kensington Palace to St James's, again the silence: the occasional cry from the crowd seemed shocking in its intrusiveness. People threw flowers into the princess's path. The captain of her guard later admitted that he had worried about how the horses would react to that, and that his men had found the 'weeping and wailing a bit unnerving'; he himself had feared 'our bearskins might get knocked off'. Yet, what we saw seemed to herald a different sort of revolution, one which used flowers, not brickbats, as its weapons and quietly contained emotion instead of war cries to make its point. The Queen herself stood in tribute, gathering her family to wait with her outside the palace gates for the coffin to pass. When did a ruling monarch last wait for a subject's passing? Something had happened in this last week to which the ruling principle itself must bow.

In the traditional way, Diana was accompanied only by men: first by her soldiers, and then, from St James's, by her sons and their father, uncle and grandfather as well. Yet as the Abbey tolled each minute of her journey this was also a very different sort of dignity. The coffin was accompanied by a small wreath of white roses and a card that said, simply, 'Mummy'. Behind the uniformed, dark-suited funeral procession walked 500 representatives of charities with which the princess had been especially concerned. They brought another energy.

How to reconcile the facets of Diana? There was no room for the charity workers in the Abbey, where the congregation witnessed that this had indeed also been a showbusiness princess. 'I Vow to Thee My Country', the congregation sang, Diana's favourite hymn, but no member of the Royal Family spoke for her. When Elton John sang 'Candle in the Wind', the boundaries between outside and inside began to dissolve. There was a sound like rain on the Abbey roof; it was the applause of those listening to the service from outside. When they heard Earl Spencer's tribute to his sister, the applause started again, much louder. And then, amazingly, it was taken up by those inside the Abbey as well.

What were they applauding? Earl Spencer had given thanks for his sister's compassion, style, beauty and intuition. He had also evoked 'a very insecure person, almost childlike in her desire to do good for others so she could release herself from deep feelings of unworthiness'. He had spoken angrily of the newspapers which had so plagued her and were the main reason for her endless talk of getting away from England. And he issued a clear challenge to the Royal Family in his pledge to Diana that the Spencers, her 'blood family', would do all they could to ensure that her upbringing of her sons continued 'so that their souls are not simply immersed by duty and tradition, but can sing openly as you planned'.

In that unprecedented spread of applause from 'the people' to the powerful and influential, to the ears of the monarchy itself, what shifted in the collective balance of psychic energy?

Afterwards, again silence. For 25 minutes at the end of the service, Londoners knew what it was like to be spared the sound of aircraft overhead. As the English oak, lead-lined coffin was driven north to the Spencer home, Althorp Park, the route was still lined with people; at one point, the hearse had to stop because the flowers thrown as it passed were obscuring the windscreen. Diana was buried in a private ceremony on an island in the estate. Here, her brother emphasised, she would face the rising sun for ever and ever. In this, at least, her grave is like that of every other Christian soul.

By then the mounds of flowers in their cellophane had begun to fester. An image: a young Scout helping with the clear-up, wearing a face mask as protection from the stench. A whiff of corruption tainted the odour of sanctity as the gossip, revelation and speculation about Diana, and later her brother, continued. People who had hardly dared, they said, to speak during that week, now found they weren't alone in thinking it had all been a bit much; immature sentimentality at best, a dangerous 'mass hysteria' at worst. The zealous pursuit of cash by the Memorial Fund opened in Diana's name turned tawdry when it endorsed a brand of margarine. Earl Spencer fell into public dissent with his sister, the fund's President, when he called for it to set a date for its own closure. Some of the people of Kensington had no wish at all to welcome up to five million visitors a year to a proposed Garden of Remembrance in their local park.

Business as usual? Yet the Memorial Fund still draws a staggering £1m a week in donations and expects to reach £100m by the end of 1998. Elton John may say enough is enough, but 'Candle in the Wind' sold almost four million copies in Britain alone within a month of its release and is still, with 31 million copies sold world-wide, the best-selling single ever. Noel Gallagher shocked an Australian audience by telling them that (expletives deleted) half the people at Diana's funeral wouldn't even visit their grandmother's grave; that's maybe not unexpected from one of the bad boys of British pop. Professor Anthony O'Hare, honorary director of the Royal Institute of Philosophy, chastised the Princess for her elevation of feeling and image over reason and restraint, and found that the week following her funeral marked a sad turn in public mores. *The Times* was moved to take him to task in a leading article. When in January 1998 bookings opened for visits to Althorp in July and August, the 200 'phonelines were jammed as an estimated 10,000 callers a minute, from all round the world, attempted to get through. People still need to find the princess, to make their devotions and be in her presence.

Had Diana lived, the dilemma of her life would have been its division – no longer a Royal Highness, yet still, as the mother of the future monarch, in the spotlight. She both illuminated the world and obscured it. Neither royalty nor private citizen, she was both patron and saint. Shortly before her death, determined to find a place of selfhood, she publicly reflected that she might be able to help resolve the conflicts in Northern Ireland. But it was only in death that she won her majority and her coronation as Queen of Hearts. When she died, the nation seemed to discover that Diana's contradictions were their own: she connected with the hidden depths of our most shallow desires and the heights of our deepest longings. Those who shared in the collective mourning occupied, like Diana's life, Eliot's space between 'the deceitful face of hope and of despair'.

As analysts, most of us believe that change is likely to occur from the inside; we prefer a culture of depth and intensity to one of surface and light. But Diana seemed to turn some of us inside out. Finding a shared meaning to the response that her death evoked became as vexing as the riddle of the Sphinx. Like a Greek chorus we, as members also of her public, bear witness to the broken rhythms of her tragic dance. In the grip of an archetypal energy, we have found a new story – that of a princess, who was also a wounded healer, and whose life embodied a collective longing for paradise. It is both history and much more. It will be told again and again, and in the retelling it will not be accuracy that matters. Rather it will be the forging of links in a chain which continues to weave, in the particularity of one life, a reflection of all others. Of this chain, this book is a part.

Diana's Diffuse Charisma

DAMIEN DOORLEY

One evening in the week before Diana's funeral cortège passed along the main roads north out of London, the subject of her death, by then more or less faded in interest, came up only a little during a supper I was having with some friends. One of them, a tetchy teacher and writer with a precise and gloomy voice that goes well with his thoughts, was saying that to compose an elegy for Diana must be especially hard. You could not find the person who had died, only a proliferation of incomplete, messy meanings. His usual poetic strategy would have been to take the individual life and turn it this way and that until it caught a universal light. In Diana's case you would have to turn the life so that dazzling collective reflections were shaded out and a person emerged. And this might come dangerously close to a psychopop summary, too much like bathos or criticism, neither eulogy nor elegy. Rather like the newspapers, in fact.

The only other conversation about Diana circled around whether anyone would go to watch her cortège pass the following Saturday. Too much like tourism, even if she was likeable, and even if she wasn't. What else would it be for? When I said I was going, since the cortege passed along the top of my road, I wondered whether anyone might evoke some notion of principled abstention as a force to head me off. But even the most political of the eaters that evening was long ago too old for this sort of daft *ad hoc* fundamentalism. She was busy getting incandescent about Germaine Greer having turned into just a bullying flirt, and Diana not being much of a model for anyone. But I didn't get any requests for sleeping over in order to beat the crowds either. Not what it used to be, this self-releasing, consciousness-raising icon business. Nobody minded much one way or the other.

But one other diner, also an analyst, said she'd felt chilled when Diana had declared on Panorama that she wanted to be the princess of people's hearts, and had believed that from that moment she'd had it.

I was thinking on the way home how detached had been the atmosphere of that evening compared to a meeting of Jungian colleagues at which Diana's death had carried a numinous significance. It was treated, I thought, like a sacrifice which had enabled a resurgence, though God knows of what. I was surprised as I listened to many of the analysts welcoming the reaction in the country, while for me it remained strange, if benign. I supposed my puzzlement might have something to do with not really getting the point. Or maybe my lack of reaction had its roots in a trace of Irish phlegm at the English aristocracy and their high jinks, even when they come to grief. Just maybe. But then the right wing press too tended to express the feeling that the country had gone mad (though they thought Diana had as well), while New Labour's sails seemed opportunistically set to catch any puff of populist feeling. I suppose if a religion doesn't grab you it just makes you wonder. There was something strange, maybe sympathetic, maybe grotesque, about this folk religion that had sprung up at the gates of Kensington Palace, and of the image of Diana as a blend of Celtic Flora and Catholic Virgin. This must be what happens to female totems, they are set up not as paternal authorities but as images of desire or mercy. The old depth psychology understanding of ambivalence seemed to be missing. That nice old cliché of radical suspicion, when I remembered it, made me think that under the public grief there might also exist the traces of a wish that after all the princess would die, and a weird gratification that things had turned out so beautifully badly.

The Saturday morning of Diana's funeral was the stillest I have experienced in a city. Not even the early shufflers after newspapers and milk disturbed the peace. Every shop was shut, as if by decree, from Waitrose and Habitat at the top of my street to the Punjabi minimart and newsagent at the bottom. Since shops have been compelled to open on the seventh day my road has been busier then than on the other six. Now it was as quiet as a village. I recognised in this odd stillness the blessed relief of one of the old Sundays. Inside we were all timing our emergence into the street by the progress of the cortège on television. When we thought the hour was right we set out and joined the stream of pedestrians in the traffic-free road, all of us heading wordlessly up the last hundred yards to the barely policed ribbon of people already in place. Tourists, voyeurs, worshippers, maybe, but in the main, witnesses. This at any rate was what I thought I was making of myself and my daughter on my shoulders. She would have a memory of something that seemed to matter, even if I had little idea why. After all, it was happening, whatever it was, at the end of our street.

And it happened quickly and quietly. Two policemen on motorbikes, outriders in black, encouraged a bewildered driver, the only person in London, possibly Europe, who didn't know what was happening, to scuttle out of the way. This profane element shooed off, the hearse slid by. I vaguely tried to register that there was the body of a famously lovely woman under the flowers and ornate wood. A few people clapped. When the small cortège had passed the crowd dissolved easily into shoppers, and we strolled home in the warm sun.

On the walk back, all the normal noise starting up again, I remembered that some years earlier I had been in a village in Belgium at the time of another royal demise. When King Baudouin died, the countryside was quiet, the village on tiptoe. The radios and televisions were on all over the house, and a noisy family usually only concerned with its own doings was subdued and oddly content. The bells of the village church, conventionally sounding the Sunday hours, made emotional sense. We all knew this is what bells are really for, to mark the death of a good and private king.

Above all Baudouin, in contrast to the Anglo Saxon crew, was private. A childless Catholic who abdicated for a day so as not to impede or endorse passage of a crucial abortion bill, and who took Gladstonian interest in the fate of prostitutes. You might have noticed him on postage stamps in the 1960s, a cross between Buddy Holly and Michael Caine, with his big glasses and his quiff, but stuck in what looked like a white metal uniform. Apart from that you would hardly have known this conflicted, principled man was there, unlike the rowdy English toffs across the sea.

Baudouin was content to look like a pop star and actor without being driven by royal vanity to compete with them. Perhaps he felt he mattered enough to his family and friends, famous among them; and if not, he was not daft enough to think he could make up for the fact that the hearts of those he loved were closed to him by finding a public route into the hearts of strangers. Since Baudouin's ordinary elderly death from illness, the Dutroux case, revealing a decade of paedophilia, child murder and grotesque police bungling, has compelled Belgium to realise it is no longer innocent, nor very mature. Baudouin, though, does not appear, so far, to have contributed to its sleaze. Unhappily in these days you hold your breath at the vulnerable spectacle of a good reputation.

This comparison, while I was puzzling over what all the fuss was about, made me wonder what makes a public figure charismatic to a very large group. Diana's charisma could point to a crucial coincidence of her aspirations and those of a public she had made her own. Many column inches have since been devoted to trying to sort out just what that coincidence might be. I remembered Ellenberger's review of Rorschach's career, (Ellenberger, 1993) one of his many invaluable disinterments in the history of psychiatry. Among other things, Rorschach (of ink blot fame) undertook a fascinating and incomplete study of Swiss sects in the Waldau region, and made some observations about the way in which they were founded and maintained.

Firstly, they tended to flourish in frontier regions. Secondly, they had two types of leaders: the passive, chosen by their group and without much influence, and the active, who declared their own prophet-like nature and enjoyed considerable prestige. Rorschach diagnosed the active leaders he met as in some cases schizophrenic. He believed the deep influence of the mentally ill prophet came from the fact that his cult contributions not only contained the 'low mythology' (ibid., p. 205) of the neurotic, founded on personal complexes, but also drew on the 'high mythology' (ibid., p. 205) of the archetypes that possessed his ego and which were deeply impressive to his disciples. Thirdly, he noted that having sex with the leader was (unsurprisingly) supposed to be spiritually beneficial. And finally he discovered among the initiated a troubling tradition of belief in the value of incest.

I also remembered the tentative argument about charisma in a paper by Aberbach (Aberbach, 1995). He thinks of charisma as to a great extent an aesthetic phenomenon, and suggests a cocktail of ingredients which makes up a charismatic person and which synchronises the emergence of their public moment. Firstly, he emphasises unresolved childhood grief, which makes the charismatic strive to create a new identity, 'a semi-mythic persona' (ibid., p. 846) through which the charismatic may create a new 'prosthetic relationship' (ibid., p. 847) with the public. This may be pathological, but is not necessarily only so. Secondly, a period of social or political disaffection is essential in providing the gap for the charismatic to enter the public arena as an icon of grievance and aspiration. And thirdly, he suggests that to the extent that the charismatic's bond to the group is founded on serious early disruption in the relationship with loved ones, the charismatic's love affair with the public can be thought of as a form of 'displaced incest' (ibid., p. 851).

Both studies seem relevant to understanding Diana's influence, which is aesthetic, religious, social and sexual.

In place of Rorschach's geographical frontier, Diana struggled to patrol the ever troubled frontiers of class, sexuality and privacy. Without doubt she has been the purveyor of a piece of Rorschach's high mythology that would be the envy of any Swiss cult leader. And, crucially, she fulfils the criterion of an active leader by her self-declaration as a new kind of royal: a disenfranchised princess trawling for a new clientele among the disaffected.

Her troubled childhood, which makes her like so many of us, fulfils Aberbach's required early unhappiness and loss. One can almost see in retrospect the painful construction of the prosthesis of diffuse love and applause, and the sadness as well as the agony of its application. And then there is the summer of 1997, and the apparent synchronising of her aspirations with those of the public. It was possible to think the country was changing in the way she would have wanted it to change, and becoming an environment better for her as well as everyone else.

No wonder she was enshrined, I thought, after looking at her this way. Still, the shrine wasn't very attractive. I thought I might get closer, breathe in some of the incense of the cult, and see if I could get high. Usually I've found the main obstacle to cult enthusiasm not to be a kind of liberal rationality, but a Catholic childhood. It can somehow leave you with the impression that even if religions don't amount to half of what they are meant to be, the old ones still failed at it best. And then there was the lucid deconstruction of charisma in Jung's essay on the mana personality (Jung, 1928), a worried prophylactic against inflation and against adherence to anyone with that seductive disease. Again, it seemed sadly apt to Diana's story, although Jung emphasises not so much the aesthetic in the case of the female mana personality as the maternal, moral, self-sacrificing image, the 'discoverer of the great love' (ibid., par. 379). As I got closer to the shrine, and re-read his paper, I was struck by the tone of warning in the way he treats the subject. 'It's a question of might against might. If the ego presumes to wield power over the unconscious, the unconscious reacts with a subtle attack' (ibid., para. 391). And after a digression in which he likens this reaction of the unconscious to that of an abused digestive system, he disavows his unpoetic and morality-free metaphor, and rounds off '. . . it would be more fitting to speak of the wrath of the injured gods' (ibid., par. 392). In a version based on Jung's view, a narrative of ego inflation avenged by the archetypes she invoked, like mortal Arachne punished by divine Athene, Diana's shrine in the public imagination may commemorate a psychic disaster.

The risky wish to be the princess of people's hearts may indeed have about it a whiff of hubris (aggression). Diana's Panorama statement was a sweet declaration of war. The monarchy wouldn't have her, so she stole their clientele. How did she do it? In part, as a renewing, aesthetic, erotic, conscience-pricking object. That is a very Sixties stab at fame, very British, and very tried and tested. It is what pop stars have learnt to do since youth and transgression became the social qualities with the most clout. But as Jung puts it later in his essay, 'The Pauline overcoming of the law falls only to the man who knows how to put his soul in the place of conscience' (ibid., par. 401). Whatever that means, it probably doesn't include a conviction that beauty, chic and disavowed aggression are enough to get by on, enough to throw in the face not only of tradition, but also in the face of evil.

There is that image of Diana strolling, beautifully slacked and bloused, along or through a minefield, wearing body armour and a visored helmet. Her pricey loafers might at any moment spring a detestable landmine. It's a clever, vexing image. In one go it can evoke anxiety, admiration and distaste. When Diana was seen on television holding the hand of an AIDS patient there was again the sense of risk and courage, which made some people hold their breaths again. To say it was staged is to miss the point, because she meant it anyway. This gesture took place in a different dimension from that of her chic stroll along the minefield. While that dangerous ground was far away in a place exotically poor and ravaged, the AIDS gesture took place in the same air its viewers breathed, and on the same ground they trod fearfully. To many the patient was an emblem of anxiety and anger, the expiring actor in a morality fable about the evils of homosexuality, or the evils of homophobia, depending. The social value of the act was that it took place in a frontier zone, not geographical like the beat of Rorschach's cult leaders, but social and sexual, a fertile wilderness for any English charismatic.

I think it's possible that such risk also involves the expiation of guilt as much as creative aggression. It would appear that self esteem is often most effectively restored through a revolutionary act, which may take the place of mourning. The attention most desired is that of the first lost object, whom the finally achieved charismatic fears they once drove away.

The social payoff from these gestures (something between public symbol and private acting out) is not to be sneezed at. Diana's charisma has a diffuse appeal, as diffuse as her own personality, creating a loosely connected complex of local, marginalised causes. She is like a bundle of those old-fashioned local saints whose shrines you come across on holiday, and whose emblems show they are the patrons of people who suffer or aspire in very precise ways. Her appeal is on the one hand global, on the other scattered and charitable.

In the same way her personal story is defined by controversy and contradiction, and has many different versions, depending on the viewer or reporter. Friends writing in the papers stated how witty and sexy she was, or how privately kind and generous. These reports mattered so much because they offered a picture quite different from that of the disturbed, selfish woman often described.

The thing is, so many narratives fit her. Here is a plausible archetypal fiction about her. In order to be loved, and maintain herself against one narcissistic blow after another, she naively invoked the numinous image of something between Aphrodite and the Virgin Mary, not thinking she was entering into a Faustian pact with archetypal reality and invoking enigmatic objects even trickier than the media. A chilling story emerged from the unconscious and lived her. The princess of people's hearts may also live out her subjects' most aggrieved suicidal selves, their pathologies of repetition. She died the obligatory young terrible death, the death of our wildest, angriest, most elegiac dreams. More Pollyanna than Persephone.

She was a kind of media Everywoman, playing this role and that. There's the one where she acts the part of the lovely, privileged girl with a habit for dodgy blokes. It's on a level glittering enough to evoke sighs of envy, and the kiss and tell emotional transactions are tawdry enough to make them recognisable. The public loves a bit of posh, no better or worse than ourselves.

Then there's the one where she does the friend who keeps messing up: happy at last, maybe pregnant again; let's hope so anyway, because the tales of wreck are getting a bit too much to listen to. Both audience and actress flag at the length of the play.

Her best part, though, was as the patient of the nation. Always in a lot of internal trouble. All to do with being dumped by her mother as a kid. And then finding a new version of the bad mother secretly shacked up with Charles in that marriage she wittily called crowded. For my own part I can't help having a feeling for the child and adolescent these things happened to, and think it likely that her bright and bumpy parabola was launched on the negative energy of that early abandonment, a child lobbed into social space. But then I would.

Nearly a year on, the charisma is fainter. The terrible, beautiful story, surfacing from its cult interest, fades into the politics of charities, and becomes something of a defining moment of the decade. One day, when he ascends to the throne, her eldest son may reap some of the rewards of Diana's charm, and a cross-generational wound in that family might be healed, along with a wound in the relations between monarchy and the public. Perhaps his generation will cherish in each family a risqué old aunt who, on wet Sundays, gets out the Sainsbury's claret and her Diana album to reminisce and tell the kids the way it used to be when there was still innocence, or audacity, or something, long since lost, that once walked large in the world; an old bright thing who resurrects the shock of the young death, and mutters darkly against that Charles and Camilla, butter wouldn't melt in their mouths.

It is impossible not to think about one another and try to understand other people. The princess, having stumbled unhappily on this impulse in a few million souls, had the genius to manipulate it. I wish I could remember that Diana, in her last accelerated phase, used the media as a public journal in which to record an autobiography in progress. And I wish I could remember that this diary flung open is really none of my business. Or that it very probably isn't.

REFERENCES

Aberbach, D. (1995). 'Charisma and attachment theory: a crossdisciplinary interpretation.' *International Journal of Psycho-Analysis*, Vol. 76, Part 4, 1995.

Ellenberger, H. F. (1993). *Beyond the Unconscious: Essays in The History of Psychiatry*, introduced and edited by Mark S. Micale. Princeton, NJ: Princeton University Press.

Jung, C. G. (1928). 'The Mana Personality', *CW 7*: 225-239. London: Routlege and Kegan Paul, 1953.

The Grip of the Daimon

MICHAEL ANDERTON

2 SEPTEMBER 1997

As I write, I feel I want to bring together my immediate thoughts and impressions, as the collective reaction powerfully emerges. Inevitably they are mixed, mutually contaminated between personal and collective, subjective and objective, inner symbolic and outer empirical. Whether any final conclusions or interpretations follow myth or reason, and at what level a balanced sense of reality may be found, these first impressions are mercurial. They seek the insights of the groundswell of unconscious and divine forces, or emerge as pragmatic musings on fate and fatalism, or as explorations of the laws of luck and chance as opposed to meaningful providence and coincidence. I shall want to reflect, modify with time, coordinate and synthesise, but these days, like the whole of Diana's life, seem to be manifesting themselves as if in a dream. Like a dream they are self-interpreting, as we awake into the encounter, inner and outer, with its own Ariadne thread of meaning. These are the first keys, and the different facets of the complex, ambivalent in their symbolism, may evolve as events turn into history.

My first impression is that there was much here on the symbolic level that we encounter in analysis, but that it was so transparently obvious that there was hardly need to analyse it. The dream told its own story, authenticated its own truth in the questions it asked, emerging into a greater rationality than the empirical facts could ever give. My thoughts went to a terrible car crash in a high speed underground tunnel in Paris. A shared vehicle speeding through life in the unconscious – especially in Paris, the city of erotic love – sped off the straight path, hit the pillars of the Establishment and ended in disaster. The immediate symbolism speaks, but I shall seek to elaborate on a deeper and broader basis, related to the wider facts and collective attitudes. My second reaction after hearing the news was to go and wake my wife, Robin, and tell her: 'Diana and Dodi are dead, killed in a car crash'. She thought a little, as the fact registered. Then, in the frenetic atmosphere that was already gathering, there came a blanket of wholesome sanity, as she said, 'Well, perhaps it was for the best'.

The Old Testament emphasised that, if the rulers were unfaithful, particularly in terms of moral turpitude, it brought the judgement of Jaweh upon the whole nation. If Israel herself were unfaithful, she got the rule she deserved. Join to that the fact that there was a change, that Sunday morning, in the Anglican liturgical cycle. From the collect for Pentecost 14, 'that Thou being our ruler and guide, we may pass through things temporal, that we finally lose not the things eternal', it moved to that for Pentecost 15, where the petition is, 'to govern the hearts and minds of those in authority and bring the families of the nations, divided and torn apart by the ravages of sin, to be subject to His just and gentle rule'. Within five minutes of the transition, the fatal accident occured. Only recently, Diana had been excluded from the Royal Family and her name removed from the state prayers.

Let us reconsider the characters. The family drama bears all the marks of a Greek tragedy. It is almost as if from birth and the events of childhood, there could not have been a very different fate. Diana's marriage was arranged by the Establishment, but the catalyst of the animus was not in the marriage, and the husband's anima projections also lay elsewhere. Diana and Charles split apart and narcissistic exhibitionism developed its own anorexic pathology. Mutual competition, in projection of personal image as well as an unresolved love triangle, led not only to Diana's life in high society, but to an element of the child returning to the father. For the lovers, there seems to have been an element of two individuals, wounded children inside, coming together as soul mates who could share some happiness. They were journeying through a fast erotic tunnel where the unconscious complexes effected their own nemesis. What if that journey had gone on? What would have been the collisions of class, creed, race and nationality? Where, perhaps, emerges the principle that out of a lesser evil may come seeds of a greater good?

The effects of the 'Greek tragedy' are transparent. A disturbed young girl seeks to love and be loved, to conform; and yet, if she has any real spirit, she must also break out and rebel. The way she did this shows a mercurial ambivalence. The element of exhibitionism as 'the star', eclipsing her husband, living the highest jet set life, cannot but be contrasted with her overt compassion for the underprivileged. This lays itself open to the charge of mixed motives which plagues the do-gooder, 'care-bears' society. Yet it is more complicated than that, because Diana's conformity with the ruling mores seems to have had behind it a rebellion against the Establishment, a desire to show it up, a desire for revenge. Through her declared compassion for the underprivileged, she conformed exactly with what some would see as the only remaining justification for the British Royal Family: the unifying of the realm by its protection of the weak as much as the strong. Yet in the glamourous intensity of her public declaration of compassion, she seized the moral high ground and upstaged the show of which she was meant to be part.

The road to hell *is* paved with good intentions and the gateway to the tree of life is only opened by eating the forbidden fruit. We are all caught between the Scylla and Charybdis of deed and motive, between the evil that turns to good and the good that turns to evil, and a higher morality that turns traditional values upside down. Diana and Dodi cannot be seen to be other than engaged in that conflict to the full, whether they are judged as child victims of the devil or divine children, saviours in a sick and ruined world. There is both a saint and a sinner in each of us, and only the ambivalence of the wounding yet healing serpent of Hermetic wisdom and the redeeming grace of God, as a part of the same mystery, can bring to our perplexity some light at the end of the tunnel.

There emerges the picture of a tortured and misguided soul, combining complexity and cunning, yet somewhere with a genuine saviour complex. Diana had a heart and yet she died of a massive heart attack: 'whatsoever ye mete, shall be meted unto you again'. Even our good deeds come back to us not only in reward but in judgement. My father spent the last years of his working life caring for disabled ex-servicemen and died in a wheelchair. An awareness can sometimes come, with overwhelming and blinding clarity, of a God who does not pussyfoot.

Why are we reacting in the ways that we are? It is as if society, in projecting its own shadow, needs not only a scapegoat, but also a vicarious saviour, hero or heroine. In the massive depersonalisation and loss of identity of the modern age , there seems to be the need for a figure through which to live the positive energies of our lives, as parents live their lives through their children. Yet all our reactions seem somewhere to fail, from the mass hysteria to the voices of the world leaders. The court historians seem to be having a field day of pitiful panacea in their smug pomposity, and church leaders are unable to be even remotely convincing. Runcie is patently contaminated by theoretical technique. Carey seems to bypass the personal tragedy to concentrate prayers not on the principal actors but on the children, in a way reminiscent of the

Church of England's official emphasis on the primacy of children, irrespective of the complex personal issues involved in the compromise of divorce. Thinly disguised, behind a grudging acknowledgement of Diana's compassion and good works, is an obvious ambivalence about the eventual salvation of the protagonists, a reflection of doctrinaire application of the puritan heresy, with all its dangers of pietistic prejudice. The phenomenon includes that which this society cannot come to terms with, namely death. We sweep it under the carpet, inviting every perverse projection. Here, all publicity was acceptable except for photographs of the injured dying.

If God has a hand in this and is the Lord of Providence, the question must arise 'Where is now your God?' Perhaps in the deep and terrible questions of faith and fate, our own faith may deepen and grow and our own share in the evolving myth of the divine destiny of our world may find greater realisation and fulfilment. We come full circle to where we started: 'Perhaps in the end, it is all for the best'. Who knows? It is important that we cannot be too sure, doctrinaire or didactic. We echo with Julian of Norwich: 'There is no hell, for all will be well and all manner of things will be well, as for the hazelnut in the palm of the hand, for God loves it'.

9 SEPTEMBER 1997

The funeral is over, but the extraordinary overflowing of emotion and recognition continues. It is a phenomenon that must eventually be judged in the perspective of history. But this seems a convenient point to make further comment and speculation, even though the watershed of integration has not yet been reached.

The archetype that we can see at work is the *daimon*. This spiritual force affects our life as a powerful influx from outside. The concept is ambivalent, for the daimon may be a force of either God or the Devil and God can appear demonic while the seductions of the Devil can have the appearance of a divine panacea. The daimon in its nature is mercurial, containing all the opposites, and it is in the matrix of the mercurial fountain, the basis of transformation in the personality, that they find their creative synthesis.

The God can be an overall value, powerful and in control, and yet create evil, break down and destroy, to remake on a higher level. The Devil can be a spanner in the works that constantly thwarts our best laid plans, but can also be the despised element that creates a lesser evil for a greater good. For our purposes, we must regard the daimon in whose grip we undoubtedly now are as both good and evil. We have had a tragedy that appears as a terrible evil:

young life cut short in its prime in a senseless accident. Yet this evil has been followed by an outpouring that promises a greater good than even Diana could have dreamed of achieving. In the middle of this, we have had a thorough shaking up of the status quo. Who at this stage can say if it is for good, or evil, or both?

In both the Christian and the Egyptian religions, the daimon was the heroic youth, struck down in the beauty of the prime of life. In the Egyptian pantheon, this divine youth or maiden goddess was essentially of the Devil, a demonic luciferian child. In Christian mythological cosmology and historical symbolism, it is the divine Son of the Father which is sacrificed. But interestingly, both sacrifices, divine and demonic, are atoning: they make whole, and are healing to individual and society. The essence of the sacrifice is that it may be imposed or voluntary. If freely accepted it is divine; if resisted it is demonic, splitting and divisive. Here, the sacrifice is free in compassion and imposed in acccident: both sides of the daimon are manifest. But even here within the ambivalence, in the spirit of the great law of sacrifice, there may be the seeds of a health-giving evolution.

Another issue again is that of unconsciousness. There is an old mystic saying: 'Man, if thou knowest what thou doest, thou are blest, if thou dost not know what thou doest, thou are damned'. Are we seeing a genuinely redeeming principle becoming conscious in both the individual and society through a sacrifice which, even if unwilled, seemed somehow inevitable? Are we possessed by an unconscious shadow projection that rejects oppression and evil, living collective hopes through the figure of a tragic heroine which gives meaning to the conflict and latent tragedy of life and a release from fear and timidity?

In our mass, depersonalised, society there is a tremendous urge for identity. The shadow must find a scapegoat and the desire for fulfillment must find a hero. We are seeing a phenomenon in which the whole body of society can relieve its discontent and lean towards an identification of all it wishes for. It is as if there is a longing for the lost glory of a nation that once ruled the world, that cast itself, whatever the ambivalence of the motive, in the role of saviour servant to all that is less fortunate in humanity. As a Spencer, Diana belonged to a family whose roots in the nation are more ancient than those of the Hanoverian monarchy. She threw herself into the role of the saviour servant – indeed, was seized by that archetype – but she used it too to stage her rebellion, with tools that were exactly those the monarchy would employ to justify its popularity. Here she becomes the thorn in the flesh, the despised element that puts to nought the things that are, as well as the enshrined saint who shakes the Establishment in its false complacency and activates the mercurial daimon that heals. We can find a mythological parallel in the Grail legend. In the figure of Diana we can see the goddess Kundry whose unbridled instinct has resulted in King Amfortas's incurable wound; we can also see, in Diana's simplicity, care and compassion, the divine fool Parsifal who breaks his spear and heals that wound. The sacrifice is complete in the symbol of the Grail vessel in her island grave, where an apotheosis of the feminine earth element is sanctified.

It is as if God has put a divine spanner in the works to shake up his creation, showing himself a God of extremes, with a terrible dark as well as a light side. But where is the obstinacy and perverseness of human nature that calls for such drastic treatment? Where are the extremes of justice and mercy, wrath and love, punishment and forgiveness, goodness and severity in a God whose divine providence is not mere fatalism but active in relation to humankind's free will and responsibility, in terms of an ultimately all-powerful will in the collective unconscious? We need the language of paradox, which must rest somewhere with unanswered questions, in a situation which we nevertheless cannot but struggle to understand.

The age in which we live is undergoing dramatic change, which, with a certain amount of speculation, seems to be mirrored astrologically. The age of Pisces, now ending, is hierarchical between leaders and led, vertical in divisions of social activity and responsibility. The coming age of Aquarius is horizontal, cooperative, and one in which individuals take more responsible authority into their own hands in the context of the whole. The movement can be seen as a new individuation process. The Platonic mould, of the men of iron who do the work and the men of silver who administer the politics of the men of gold who determine the rule, is all taken into the self-determining individual, who in turn is integrated into a cohesive, evolving whole.

For now, we are in a state of flux, with all the birth-pangs and perversions of the process. Divisions are not only healed but also seem to get wider in terms of money, power and humankind's inhumanity – to itself. As we come to the end of the age of Pisces there are the two fishes: the Christ and the anti-Christ. Never has the conflict seemed greater; we seem to live in apocalyptic times. But where the greatest danger is, there is the greatest potential for redemption. It is perhaps not strange that the old and the new should meet in the mass globalism and dehumanisation of a material consumer society from which we cannot retreat, but can only seek to understand and redeem. In this tragedy, there is a mirror of archetypal events in spiritual world history: there is an echo of the Christ's gospel of liberation to the poor and oppressed at the stable door of existence, and of the Buddha's vision of compassion for suffering humanity. There is the age-old problem of poverty and riches, class and breeding: the Christ was of the royal line of David and the Buddha embraced poverty from a noble family of rulers. The shake-up of established values since the war has brought us to an age of irreligion in which the alternative society is showing a considerable element of religious revival. In many ways, the world has never been sicker and yet never had a greater potential.

Such times have always invited the visitation of the daimon. It may come from without, but the germ seed is within. In the current upsurge of energy the seeds of divine grace and revelation may be seeking a new fruition. If this is not to become demonic possession and a mass psychosis – which always happens when the collective takes over the individual – each of us must take the seed back into ourselves. In the daimon, in our own shadow and light, we may then evolve in our deepest being and in our collective community and society.

A Princess 'More Sinned Against than Sinning'?

JANE HAYNES

These lines, spoken by King Lear, and often used as an A level examination question, with the addition of the instruction, 'Discuss', will now resonate in relation to Diana, at different levels, in almost every ear. In death, if not in life, Diana has proved herself to be an archetypal tragic victim, whose death has constructed a national catharsis. As Jungian analysts we have been privileged to witness the archetypal processes of the secular canonisation of a saint before our eyes. The mixture of hysteria with sexuality and saintliness are familiar. Richard Crawshaw writes of St Teresa (canonised in 1622):

> Scarce had she learnt to lisp the name
> Of Martyr . . .
> She never undertook to know
> What death with love should have to doe;
> Nor has she e're yet understood
> Why to show love, she should shed blood
> Yet though she cannot tell you why,
> She can Love and she can Dy. (Bennett 1966, p. 106).

Roy Foster, Professor of Irish History at Oxford, comments on how the measure of our self-identification reaches even further back into the utopian 'Never Never Land' of fairy tale. Foster discusses how: 'The structural analyst of folk-tales Vladimir Propp demonstrated the restricted number of forms and functions on which a fairy tale was based and Diana's life fulfilled many of them: the absent mother on a remote island, the wicked step-mother (who even arrived at the funeral dressed like Cruella de Ville), the Cinderella-existence as nursery helper – and then the transformation-scene that led to the Palace, the glass coach and a new story' (Foster, 1997). At first this new story remained faithful to its genre: At a gala charity Washington ball for breast cancer research in June 1997, Diana, the Queen of Broken Hearts, dressed in bridal white, chose and read aloud the following lines by an Australian poet: 'Life is mostly froth and bubble,/Two things stand like stone:/Kindness in another's trouble,/Courage in your own'.

It seemed that anyone who had experienced a broken love affair could identify with Diana's wounds, from which charisma and manna flowed. From time to time there were shadow emanations but they were quickly absorbed by the devotion of her global audience. Nevertheless, to the discerning eye, Diana's preoccupations with death and darkness were also constant. Her preference for dark male figures, who embodied the Stranger archetype rather than captains of the guard, first emerged in the form of the dedicated and introverted heart surgeon from Pakistan, who couldn't, or wouldn't, endure the intrusions of privacy and constant media exposure. In an interview in *Vanity Fair* with Tina Brown last June, Diana was asked if she would ever marry again: 'Who would take me on, I have so much baggage. Anyone who takes me out to dinner has to accept that their business will be raked over in the papers and photographers will go through their dustbins. I think I am safer alone'.

Only weeks later Diana had found an unsafe partner who relished the lime-light every bit as much as she did. Diana the insider, bluer than blue, and Dodi the outsider, born into the dark Egypt of Naguib and Nasser, who succeeded the deposed playboy King Farouk. Their tragic *folie à deux*, which was consummated in death, was accompanied by obscene and graphic media details of fatal injuries and voyeurism. These brutal and mindless acts which have been described by Salman Rushdie as 'a sublimated sexual assault' which departed from the familiar resolution of fairy tale genre and resonated better to J. G. Ballard's novel *Crash*. This new narrative has reflected uncomfortable and denied truths about the collective erotic imagination.

In the short space of this essay, written in the month after the funeral, I do not only want to capture Diana's death with a Jungian lens, despite the appropriateness of its aperture, but rather to give ear, with the permission of the analysands that I quote, to the range and intense depth of affects the event precipitated in them. I cannot speak of my own intensity because there was none to speak of. The only distress that I felt, other than the distress I feel for any of the unknown who leave home and are, as a result of fatality, pre-vented from returning, was for the motherlessness of the two princes; my heart went out to the particular difficulties of their specific tragic circumstances. Otherwise, I have felt as much for a motherless and dying fledgling as I have for the *physical* loss of Diana.

Yet her death seems to have facilitated an instant New Labour national education programme in mourning. It made it possible for hundreds of thousands of people, who hitherto may have found it easier to shed a tear over Bambi's loss of mother, to transfer their own insufficiently acknowledged and repressed fears of loss and death onto Diana's ambiguous and seemingly divine form. Suddenly it became possible, in the collective processes of national mourning, for individuals to lose their separateness, merge, and thereby pass over into the universal. One of the most extraordinary facets of this national mourning process has been the declaration of the People that they felt, not *as if* but that they *concretely* knew Diana.

During the week after the Princess's death, I came to terms with the fact that for approximately 35 hours my consulting room was filled with an unique outpouring of affects and responses to a tragedy that superseded almost every other personal preoccupation. It was also filled with an ugly shadow which took the forms of Rumour, Chinese Whispers and Gossip about the perverse activities of members of the Royal family which are obstructed from tabloid comment by prohibitive D notices. And I have to admit that my pulse also quickened.

One of my analysands had, in the week preceding Diana's death, discovered that her wedding, scheduled for mid-September, had to be cancelled because her fiancee's *decree nisi* had been deferred. She began the following session:

First of all I have to put all my own problems aside and speak about Diana because I am shocked by how affected I have been. It has been forced upon me from the outside, and I don't like that, but it has led me to think what do I really believe about my life, it has led me to think of God, not God with a beard but what's really great and small, how small and unprotected our lives really are and how powerful death really is. I haven't been able to say this, except to you, but I think Diana had nowhere else to go, it was a wonderful release for her, it was inevitable that she would increasingly become a public nuisance, and she has been spared that deterioration in her image. If she did good, and she did, it was accidental to the central core of her life, but her life wasn't motivated by good deeds, she sought her reflection in them. Her death has served her life and the people in a way that living could never have done. I find myself thinking – out of nowhere, thinking of the prayer of St Francis of Assisi, 'Let me be instrumental in thy peace'. The crowds are thinking differently, they are thinking more femininely, there's a people's philosophy abroad even though it's heavily tainted with sentimentalism, it's better than mugging, drugs and violence.

A difference I have found between male and female voices is that the men have been more reluctant to let me know how preoccupied they are. Yet a quick reckoning reveals that more of my male analysands referred to visiting the Palaces than females. On the Monday morning after her death, one of my male analysands, who wears only designer jeans, turned up dressed like one of the ravens at the Tower. As it transpired, he made no reference to Diana whatsoever, and I was left none the wiser about the conscious meaning of his blackness. The following session he did make a prolonged and distressed reference to the funeral and I was able to refer back to the paradox. He looked at me in some bewilderment and said, 'Did you say I was dressed in black? How extraordinary, I have absolutely no recall of such a thing, not even now that you mention it. Are you quite sure?' I proceeded to describe his garments, which he acknowledged as owning. Then he said:

But it would have been quite impossible for me to talk about Diana then, I have been in mourning all week, and it is only now that I can trust myself to talk about it without losing control.

Another male analysand struggled half way through his session before sheepishly turning to the Diana myth. I quote from the Tuesday session after her death. By now we were halfway through and I thought no reference to Diana would occur. He was talking about how he had attended a professional engagement with some of the leaders of the Orangemen in Ireland over the weekend, but then he said:

And that's where I heard the news about Diana's accident. One of the leaders of the Orangemen turned to me and said 'That's what happens if you consort with the Devil.' I thought what precisely does he mean? The literal devil? Dodi? The media? And then I started thinking about Presbyterianism and my own roots. The straight and narrow path that I was always being preached as a boy, and which I have abjured. This Diana business has turned into a myth, but it's a myth without roots. She was essentially a woman without resources but the media became her resource. Somewhere she or someone knew the references to Christ, but it forced me to think more importantly about my own losses or gains – this great sense of loss is imposed on one from the outside but for me it becomes another model of self evaluation. I find myself having to talk about it here, no-one can resist it. Diana's a Barbie saint, we have a bonanza of mourning. Yes, you're right to talk about shrines and pilgrimages, as the people become aware of what it is that they have lost, just like Jesus. I was taken aback when I turned on the news this morning and learnt that all sports events had been cancelled, they have been rescheduled for Sunday, suddenly Sunday becomes secular by comparison with Diana's Day. Diana's promiscuity has quickly been forgotten by the public and so the secular becomes divine. I was discussing it all with a professor of media studies yesterday and her view was that Diana was a girl without any education, she'd grown up without Jane Austen, Brontë and Eliot, and she didn't like sports, so she came to the job without any resources, that is until she discovered the media.

(I was subsequently interested to note that in an interview in *The Observer*, 21 September, Sue Townsend also refers to the Princess as 'a fatal non reader'). Then he said: 'Goodness, it's time to go.'

As A gathered his belongings and our eyes met at the door, I felt that we regarded each other sheepishly, as though we had been caught out. And I was, indeed, thinking how unusual it was that we had both indulged in such a collective and frivolous discussion. A's actual words were: 'Hopefully it will fade by our next session'. But it didn't. We have both come to realise that it has given birth to all sorts of philosophical issues that are specific to our era of global communications.

The extraordinary extent to which my female analysands between the ages of 34 and 38 had privately taken Diana as a role model also became evident. They all remembered her engagement in detail and seemed, in the most unlikely ways, to have lived with her as an invisible companion for years. One of these women confessed that she had held secret conversations with Diana on a regular basis for years, and another otherwise radical young woman took me by surprise: 'It's quite extraordinary but we share a birthday and she's always been over my shoulder. I'm always measuring myself against her, it has helped me with my own problems when I've failed, knowing how difficult things have been for her'.

My first analysand on the Monday morning after the news of Diana's death was another such woman whom I shall refer to as B. Unlike Diana she is, despite being exceptionally attractive, unattached and more importantly in her own narrative, childless. She is professionally successful, but still recovering from a long liaison with a married man which ended three years ago and who pressurised her to abort their foetus. This precipitated a severe, although concealed, clinical depression with significant suicidal intentions:

It has been a very sad weekend for me with Diana dying, I identified with her in so many ways. There was only a day between our birthdays and we were the same age. Also there was all this publicity about the Lighthouse Trust, and then I had a phone call to inform me that the coordinator of the Buddy project I worked on had died. I knew he had AIDS but I had no idea he was so ill and I had only spoken to him a few weeks ago.

At this point I expressed some surprise that she had not told me she had found the time, in her busy professional life, to undertake such demanding voluntary commitments. 'Yes I was a Buddy for three years, to Gaia and Jo, I was with them both when they died, but it became too harrowing for me and I had to stop.' This information also took me by surprise, because B has no professional experience of dealing with sickness or the dying.

So there was this link with Di, but I also identified with her because I thought that maybe she had an abortion. I had heard on the grapevine that the press all knew about it but were not allowed to report it, she'd had to go to America. That's why she was making all those phone calls to her lover and it brought back all the pain of my abortion, and now I have suddenly and belatedly become furious with C (her ex-lover). It's taken all this time, and Diana's death. I feel as though I don't want to speak to him ever again – of course I will. After years of silence, of keeping it a secret from everyone, even you for a long time, I want to tell the world. I won't of course, telling you has now made a big difference, but the secret was locked inside of me like the baby.

I identified in my AIDS work with Di, and I've lost personal friends through AIDS but like Di I am drawn to suffering and the sick, I am always the first to answer a call, I don't mean to make myself sound good, I don't know what it means, what is it in me that makes me care so much about others? And then when I saw Prince Charles and her sisters, after they brought back the body, I just knew that I would never carry out my own suicidal feelings, not to leave people in that terrible state. But I had a dream last night about my mother. She was on a plane and she knew there was something terribly wrong with that plane, but she never said goodbye to me, and I knew she would never want to do a thing like that. It was my mother who rang yesterday and said 'Have you heard the news?' I suppose the dream was about my fear of death, everyone's fear, death is just there, no-one can escape it.

At this point she dissolved into tears. After some minutes she was able to say 'It's OK I'm beginning to feel better. That's one of the things I've discovered here, I can be unhappy, even distraught, and then recover before I have to leave'.

During the course of the week several other young women shared their identifications about the princess, which were usually focussed on their current preoccupations, with me. Returning to my consulting room after a lunch time walk I was surprised by an ex-analysand, who had moved to the area. She had seen me in the distance and come running up behind me. I was pleased to see her, but soon discovered, to my dismay and decreasing tolerance, that she too wanted to share her feelings about Diana:

I have a candle and photograph to send her on her way. When she got married it was three in the morning in Canada. My mum woke us up, she had prepared an English cream and strawberry tea! She said, 'You will never see anything like this again.' I come from the Commonwealth – a picture of the Queen hung in every classroom, it was depressing, but I loved Diana from the day I set eyes on her, she was so different.

In the course of her describing these feelings to me in increasing detail, and I have fond memories of her narrative skills, I found my reaction far more extreme than when I am working. I could barely restrain myself from imploring her to stop what felt like an assault on my shrinking inner space.

The last analysand of the week arrived, and her expression was like a storm weather warning: 'I feel like your end of the week patient. I've been so sad, so utterly sad all week'. At this point she dissolved into unfamiliar tears. Despite her often voiced feelings of depression, even despair, I have rarely witnessed her free-flowing tears. 'Yes, of course it's about Diana, I didn't realise how affected I could be, but it's also about my own loneliness. Me. I am afraid if I start to cry for my loneliness I won't be able to stop – ever.' I also experienced some silent discomfort as to whether there was anything I could contribute that would comfort her, but decided to remain silent, endure and wait with her tears. Towards the end of the session we briefly talked of other things and then she said, with a generous smile, 'I am beginning to feel better, nothing has changed except that you listened to my loneliness and I found out that I could stop crying'.

In conclusion I would like to make a comparison between the 'People's' discontent with its monarchy and its interpretation of the Queen's refusal to return to the citadel to share publicly in the cosmic state of national mourning, with Coriolanus' ordeal:

> I heard him swear . . . never would he
> Appear i' th' market place, nor on him put
> The napless vesture of humility;
> Nor showing (as the manner is) his wounds
> To th' people, beg their stinking breaths. (Act 2, 1, ll. 129–233).

Diana was different. Diana, stripped of her royal title, became the 'Princess of Hearts and The People'. She was collectively perceived as moving among the 'constituency of the rejected'. Unlike Coriolanus and the Windsors, she bared her wounds to public scrutiny. I would designate her the Princess of Narcissism who became the embodiment of a fragmented self of the post-traditional social order who sought for one of many reflections amongst the rejected and dying. One who literally wore her self on her sleeve.

As a consequence of her celluloid beauty, her suffering, her curiosity and generosity and more bizarrely, often disinhibited and feckless disclosures of self-destructing behaviour, she won the devotion of the body politic. It remains to be seen whether she will have permanently shifted the emotional complexion of a national identity.

I wrote the preceding essay at the end of the week immediately after Diana's funeral and my primary intention was to record one of the most extraordinary weeks of my professional life. When I heard of Diana's death, less than two hours after the first reports were broadcast, it never occurred to me that I would spend the subsequent week listening to one analysand after another abandon their immediate problems as they became absorbed in the arrangements for the funeral and the meanings of their reactions to it. Although I do not normally keep notes of sessions, on this occasion I requested my analysands' permission to keep a diary of the week. Immediately after a session I would try to recall verbatim their thoughts. I became witness to a collective process of mourning from which I felt emotionally exiled. Furthermore I felt that with the exception of one analysand, who shared my cynicism, the others would be dismayed if they discovered that I couldn't actively participate in their grief. At no time did I doubt the genuineness of feelings, rather I wondered where their origins lay. Rightly, or wrongly, I have since come to regard their collective body of grief as a release, or emanation, of mourning rites from the collective unconscious that have almost disappeared from our post-traditional society.

No longer do parish bells toll for the ordinary dead and the domestic arts of laying out a corpse are almost extinct. How many people have kept vigil beside a dead body and how many children could give you a definition of a shroud? When the actress Sarah Miles described how she allowed her husband's body to remain in their bed for some days after his death and her relief at the unseasonal coolness of the weather, many people thought that she was mad: But I was moved and hoped that when someone I loved died, I too would be able to keep vigil by their body, rather than experience their corpse as instantly contaminated. You have only to dwell, for less than a moment, on the domestic and social activity in Poussin's final death-side painting in *The Seven Sacraments* to recall the now extinct busy-ness of death.

In trying to understand my own lack of response to Diana's death and funeral, I was also aware that I had recently completed a long and meaningful process of mourning and for the first time understood its privileged pain. Many people who were interviewed in the park on the day of Diana's funeral referred to their own incomplete, submerged or aborted attempts at mourning. One middle aged woman spoke for many: 'I lost my mother when I was fifteen – now with Diana's death, and all this company, I can go through the processes I couldn't go through then because I was protecting other people. I was protecting my brother'. It seems that the crowds who gathered gave permission, protection and comfort to each other.

In the subsequent months I have had time in which to consider whether I have found any personal significance in Diana's untimely death. My cynicism has changed into awe; *awe* at the psychic energy that was invested in a collective longing whereby social alienation would be transformed into a great chain of being. But daydreams and fantasies alone do not transcend the drudgery that is also at the foundation of any quest for shifts in consciousness. When I reflect on the princess it is usually in the context of my work as a therapist. When I think of Diana now I no longer only think of her as the Princess of Narcissism (and I do not intend my reference to narcissism to be only derogatory), but rather as a would-be Wounded Healer. James Hillman says that the wounded healer is never *only* a person who has been hurt and can empathise, 'which is never enough to heal'. He makes an important distinction between the person who, as a result of their wounds, develops a particular ability to empathise with others who have suffered similarly and the metabolism of an altered state, or shift in consciousness, that is required by a professional therapist. ' This kind of consciousness refers to mutilations and afflictions of body organs that release the sparks of consciousness in these organs, resulting in an organ or body-consciousness. Healing comes then ... from a consciousness breaking through dismemberment' (Hillman, 1991, p. 117).

As I refer to this quotation by Hillman, I am struck by the way in which Diana's struggles with psychic dismemberment become captive in the terrible emblem of the leaden and death-mangled vehicle, almost at the dark moment when the sun was eclipsed by ash-heavy Uranus, Mars and Pluto. I am also struck by the ways in which some aspects of Hillman's descriptions, written in 1979, of the *Puer/Puella* personality were to become prophetic of Diana's sufferings and death; he even identified their susceptibility to fatal car accidents! Hillman reminds us of what myth tells us again and again, of the relationship between the wounds of the Puer archetype and flowers. Narcissus and Hyacinthus are recalled to mind: '. . . they are flower-people who are unable to bear the suffering of their own meaning through to the end . . .' (Hillman, ibid, p. 27). From Diana's wounding a flower-harvest was born. 'Through their wounds these God figures are recognised as divine, so that entry into the God's love is through the divine wound, a mimesis of the archetypal infirmity, which paradoxically gives power, as the Christian mystics so triumphantly declared' (Hillman, ibid, p. 111).

When I consider my identifications with Diana, they exist only insofar as the origins of my decision to become a therapist lay in my initial attempts to lick my wounds and soothe my own psychic dismemberment. Hillman also draws our attention to the curious connection between '*puer* persons and the vocation to therapy' and Diana was a *puer* personality. I am not sure whether one decides to become a therapist and then acquires a professional training, or whether one acquires a professional training and then, if one is genuinely gifted, *becomes* a therapist. (And the Greek origin of the word therapy means to heal). But I do know that having patients is no guarantee of becoming a therapist. And by what criteria or research do we, as a profession, evaluate our therapeutic success? Yet when we read that Diana, in her quest to find the lineaments of internal comfort, was constantly seeking out new therapies, mediums and healers, how many analysts do not raise a contemptuous eyebrow, as though our own methods of calling upon ancestral spirits were scientifically fool-proof? At what moment is any princess, analysand, or patient (and it is interesting that some people prefer the symmetry of the title of analysand and others are determined, from the start, to transfer responsibility and become a patient), liable to discover that their wounds have coalesced into the primitive beginnings of a healing formula . . .

27 MAY 1998

I am sitting with a young woman who has brains, beauty and an inheritance of wealth and traumatic losses, which include the unexpected death of her mother last year, leaving her aged twenty and orphaned. She dissolves into tears and complains:

The only thing I can do is paint and that feels so useless. I don't only want to be thick, rich and decorative, I want to do something serious. I imagine that if only I could find a way of making other people feel better, then I might be able to begin to feel better myself. I feel so ugly inside. If I could look in the mirror and instead of picking at my complexion say Hello! The lights would go on inside my head, someone would be at home instead of this emptiness.

When she recovered from her tears she said: 'Perhaps that is how Diana felt when she wanted to dissolve like a dispirin and disappear'. I am aware that whilst she has been sobbing I have an almost irresistible wish to comfort her by moving to the couch and holding her crumpled form. But I almost never use physical contact in my consulting room and remain seated, limiting my physical actions to eventually whizzing the Kleenex across the floor, despite the fact that my nose is running too. I hope that she will intuit somehow, before she leaves that there are two of us crying in the room, even though my cry is silent. And then I find myself thinking about Diana. It is time for the session to end, but the thoughts I am having are primarily syntonic with my analysand's mood.

I recall a description of Diana in *The Guardian* (26 January 1998) by Patrick Jephson, former courtier and adviser to the Princess: 'It was like watching a slowly spreading pool of blood seeping out from under a locked door'. I find some comfort in the thought that my patient can unlock her drawbridge and let me in. But ever since Diana died I have been thinking about touch. During those much televised days between Diana's death and the funeral the word 'touch' came up repeatedly: 'she had the common touch'. Again and again those interviewed associated Diana with touch, the *healing* touch. Diana was the only female member of the royal family who disdained to wear gloves when she was in contact with the public. And when the mourners were not remarking on her powers of touch they spoke of her great love of giving and receiving. Like Bottecelli's *Three Graces*, Diana became an emblem of reciprocity. In the hours of television documentaries that were subsequently made I discovered that as a child, Diana longed to be touched and hugged.

She was the six-year-old comforter of her small brother's lonely night-grief when their mother, Frances, who had given birth to five children in ten years in order to secure a male Spencer heir, ran away without warning. Although her mother, now Mrs Shand Kydd, filed for the custody of her children who 3had been at the centre of her life since she was nineteen, and although it was already customary for custody to be awarded to the mother, her own mother, Lady Fermoy, testified against her and an enforced separation began. But there is a poignant link between Diana's childhood loss of her mother and her last Will and Testament in which she reinvests her mother, through the powers of executor (shared with Commander Patrick Desmond) and more tellingly the guardianship of her grandchildren, with the maternal role of which she was legally deprived of regarding her own children's upbringing: 'Should any child of mine be under age at the date of the death of the survivor of myself and my husband I appoint my mother and my brother Earl Spencer to be the guardians of that child and I express the wish that should I pre-decease my husband he will consult with my mother with regard to the upbringing, education and welfare of our children'.

Throughout her childhood and schooling it seems that Diana animated the archetype of the abandoned child who longs to help others whilst its silent expression cries out for the loving care it cannot provide itself. Such children are often able to feed others through their own wounding whilst starving for love themselves. As an adolescent it seems that Diana's intuition was harnessed into a technique, when her voluntary service teacher taught her about the importance of touch, eye contact and accessibility when she attended to the sick and elderly.

The public's disclosure of its collective hunger for the healing touch has led me to reconsiderations, although not explicit changes, of my own technique. The question of whether there are ever exceptions when it is appropriate to abandon our Eleventh Commandment, 'Be abstinent of touch' and make physical contact in the consulting room is immensely complex. One can be seduced into thinking that Diana's healing touch is what is missing from our analytic practice, but that would be an oversimplification. The work that analysts do, when it works, is so powerful that we actually do need the white gloves that Diana abandoned. Touching psyches, as John Donne described, carries its own divinity:

> Our souls – which to advance their state
> Were gone out – hung 'twixt her and me.
> And whilst our souls negotiate there,
> We like sepulchral statues lay; (Quiller-Couch, 1957, p. 233).

But it is also important to acknowledge that the analytic decree of abstinence, which denies physical contact in any context, can impose its own sacrifice on our humanism. There are some people who find it almost intolerable, so analysts may need to think more about how sensitive our patients are to the ways in which we receive, listen and engage with them. Yet, as imaged by Donne, there are other ways in which psyches can be touched which do not entail physical contact. Even a fleeting gaze of eyes can have a power which bypasses word and gesture, while the human voice can be the most moving instrument in the world.

Do we as analysts think enough about such issues? Is it possible to teach a trainee how to use their eyes and voice, or do the origins of such talents emerge from the depths of our interiority? Diana's teacher may have instructed her in social etiquette, but she was not responsible for the expression in her eyes, or the intensity of her longing to reach out and be received. The sources of such intensity and creativity were private. The public responded to Diana because she was more accessible and human than other members of the Windsor household. One of the mourners interviewed in the

BBC's documentary *The Shrine*, whose thoughts were frequently echoed, described how 'her imperfections were what made her whole', and this made me think how often analysands complain that they experience their analysts as aloof, two dimensional, or lacking any *middle*. I think it is ironic that as a profession we spend so much time worrying about our patients' depleted inner worlds and yet live in fear of making any *carefully deliberated* disclosures about our selves, or souls. Small talk may or may not have a time and place in the consulting room, but I think it is almost always a mistake to banish common courtesy in favour of a depth interpretation. It is a necessary truism to recall that when analysands are asked what it is that they remember about their analyses, it is almost never the interpretations but rather those *unanalysed and blemished* moments when they may have experienced us as whole.

REFERENCES

Bennett, J. (1996). *Five Metaphysical Poets*. Cambridge University Press.
Dover Wilson, J. (ed.) (1960). *Coriolanus*. Cambridge University Press.
Foster, R. (1997). 'After Diana'. *The New Statesman*, 13 September.
Hillman, J. (1991). *Puer Papers*. Dallas, Texas: Spring Publications.
Quiller-Couch, Sir A.(ed.) (1957). Donne. 'The Ecstasy' in *The Oxford Book of English Verse*. Oxford: Clarendon Press.

Her Body Politic

ANDREW SAMUELS

Psychotherapists have always wanted to explore the social world and current events. It is not a new fad or fashion. Freud (1920) hoped to understand 'the riddles of the world', and Jung (1946) said that therapists 'cannot avoid coming to grips with contemporary history'. But the world never really turned up for its first therapy session. Maybe the world knew what it was doing, because many attempts to link psychotherapy and social issues have tried to make everything exclusively psychological, thereby keeping the therapist above the fray. Attempts to put politicians or other significant figures on the couch as patients have, quite rightly, been criticised and ridiculed.

It is crucial not to muddle up what goes on within an individual, such as Diana, with what happens on the much more complex level of society. Provided such errors are avoided, psychotherapy can be seen as a useful and imaginative tool of social criticism, rather than as self-indulgent psychobabble. Temptation to analyse prominent people in public can (and should) be resisted and working partnerships made with people in other areas – social policy, education, the media and environmentalism. Therapists must also recall that not everything is rosy in their own professional politics and avoid giving an impression that they have all the answers.

There is no place for psychotherapy in politics on its own, in splendid isolation. Everything depends on achieving sufficient acceptance for its perspectives, so as to achieve a situation where many policy committees and commissions would quite naturally have a therapist sitting on them, at one end of a spectrum of experts which has statisticians at the other end. We should not think in terms of committees of therapists.

On some social issues that psychotherapy addresses, you would expect to find therapists having a collective view and something to offer: for example, family life, personal relationships and communication between the sexes. The newspaper columns are full of discussions about whether and how men can be nurturing figures in family and society, and the extent to which positive political alliances between men and women are possible. And now that all responsible therapists agree that homosexuality is not a perversion or mental illness, the influential role of psychotherapy in achieving lesbian and gay rights should not be underestimated.

But there are also some hard areas of policy that, surprisingly and increasingly, are being examined from a psychotherapeutic point of view. Many people, for instance, believe in sustainable economic development, but say that it cannot happen without great numbers of people giving up many features of their comfortable lives. To achieve this, it is rightly said, requires a huge value shift. What would drive such a shift, or set limits on it, if not human psychology and human nature? Here, psychologists have a chance to present a balanced view of human nature that, while not denying greed and competitiveness, also speaks with some authority about benevolence, altruism and our desire to make something happen on the basis of our need for connectedness with others.

Another issue that is equally pressing is racial and ethnic prejudice. Without reducing such a topic exclusively to psychology ('projection' of one's unwanted bits onto another group), psychotherapists can work with activists in the minority communities to devise strategies for empowerment from within those communities, and for more effective communication with an (intolerant) majority community.

In fact, in any area of social life where there are conflicts, tensions and a potential for violence, the body of knowledge held by psychotherapy can be extremely useful and, in several conflict prevention and resolution programmes, is already being used. Phrases like 'emotional literacy' or 'emotional intelligence' are ubiquitous these days and, since Diana's death, the trend has intensified. But there is more to these words than something to do with the private side of life. The most effective political leaders (such as Tony Blair, Bill Clinton and Diana herself) and commentators have already sensed that in *fin-de-siècle*, feminist-influenced Western societies, the political has become highly personal. Stressing the value of emotional literacy in the public sphere, and taking this message to schools and colleges, is a way of convincing disillusioned young people that involvement in politics is not going to be irreversibly damaging to their sense of personal integrity.

In what follows, there is not one jot of analysis of Diana as a person or as a 'patient'. I have made a conscious attempt to link up with diverse disciplines such as political theory and gender studies, in order to ground my work, not in the all-knowing certitude and maddening rectitude of the analyst, but in the intricate cut and thrust of cultural and academic debate. There is no attempt here to position psychology and psychotherapy as foundational. They have to compete for their place in the sun (see Samuels, 1989).

I would like to focus on three issues. First, on 'Diana' as *a political phenomenon*, asking whether her death could be seen in any way as contributing to a significant moment of political change or revolution. Secondly, I am interested in speculating about *how national and indeed international emotional moods build up in society*, how they develop and transmit in culture. Third, I want to look at a whole cluster of issues that the iconic reading of 'the Princess of Wales' suggests to me around *the body, sexuality, maternity and femininity*.

In many countries, not just in Britain, there is a desire for something like a political rebirth or political transformation at the time of the millenium. The irresistible extent of Labour's electoral victory in Britain was part of that and I shall return to Tony Blair's Prime Ministerial role in relation to Diana later in this piece. Over a year on from that victory and about a year on from Diana's death, we see disappointment emerging in relation to both events. The wise – or pseudo-wise – say this was bound to happen. They bring their 'evenly hovering cynicism' to bear on politics. However, I see this as a pseudo-maturity stemming from a supercilious disengagement from the world. True maturity resides in an engagement which is open to and prepared to work with disappointment, seeing it as our problem, not Blair's or Diana's problem (Orbach, 1998).

Yet there was, and remains, a desire for political change, rebirth and transformation, and as everybody knows, change requires death and sacrifice. We got the death and we had the necessary sacrificial victim. Diana radiated what is perhaps the most salient characteristic of being a sacrifice: she was led into peril without having full knowledge of that peril. In the deepest sense, she did not know what she was doing, and this perspective is a counterbalance to the image of her as one who manipulated the press, men, and us, the public. Victims who do not know what is going on seem much more suited to become centres of a cult than those who know what they are doing.

So the conditions for a cult were there. The word cult, etymologically, is associated not only with the Latin *cultus*, which has to do with worship, but also with *collere*, to attend to, to cultivate and to respect. There is something here to consider about the necessity of a cult arising around someone to whom one wishes to attend and respect. This may be the deeper aspect of people's reactions to Diana as an unusual blend of victim (requiring attendance) and princess (requiring respect).

We wanted change, change required rebirth, rebirth required death and death required a victim. Yet nothing in politics or economics or society or indeed the world has changed at all. Social relations remain as they were. Maybe this is just how things are in politics. In the short term, nothing much changes and we will only know later if the collective reaction to Diana's death was significant. Freud's concept of *Nachträglichkeit* is relevant here. It is translated by Strachey as 'deferred action', but is more accurately rendered as 'afterwardsness' or by the French '*après-coup*' (Stanton, 1992). We do not know whether such and such an event in the past was traumatic or otherwise significant until it is later revealed to be so. We do not yet know whether anything will change as a result of the cult around Diana's death, so whatever its significance will be, it will be '*après-coup*'.

There is also what I call the ' political aspirational atmosphere' to consider. What does a group of people, such as a society, aspire to? In Jungian language we can ask: where is the Self of such a group leading the group? Changes in the aspirational atmosphere have always been part of socio-economic change and yet hard-nosed social scientists do not have the vocabulary to talk about this, nor the experience of knowing how these psychological processes unfold.

Sometimes the aspirational atmosphere is indicated by collective images and often these images cluster around the primal themes of life: sex, birth, parents, death. Something extraordinary happened in the national primal scene (the image we have of our parents' intimate life) when Diana died. She and Tony Blair became for a moment the world parents of the British nation. The inhabitants of the British nuptial chamber were the Prime Minister and the dead Princess. It was a powerfully numinous parental union and, from the standpoint of electoral politics, the reason why Blair got unprecedentedly high popularity ratings at the time of her death. This pairing was highly unusual because political systems do not often throw up harmonious pairings. For example, Margaret Thatcher never had an equal 'consort' in political or any other terms. In the United States, when it started to look in 1992 as if Hilary Clinton was becoming one half of a shared presidency, there was implacable collective hostility to the idea because people could sense just how unstoppable such a pair would be. When Diana died, the pairing just happened before anyone could stop it, and so we had a novel, public, primal scene.

The primal scene is, for me, the most political of all images (Samuels, 1994, pp. 167–70). It is the term used in psychoanalysis to refer to the relationship in the mind between the man and the woman that created the subject. The primal scene is a mixture in most of us of memory and fantasy that gets elaborated and multi-layered over a lifetime. Think about the intimate relationship of your parents or, if you grew up in a lone parent family, of the sexual life of the parent with whom you grew up. What are its characteristics? What is the image that comes to mind? What are the emotional themes of your primal scene? Is it harmonious? Is it vigourous? Is there a sharing of power, or is there an imbalance? Is the bedroom door closed? Primal scene themes are the most political themes in the internal family that one can imagine. Think of the child's sense of exclusion – and then think of political discourse about marginal, dispossessed and excluded groups in society. Or the child's curiosity – the first investigative journalism that we do. Then there is the question of who initiates and who sets the manifesto for sexual behaviour.

Concerning psychosexual politics, the Midrash tells us that before Eve was created there was Lilith. God created Adam and Lilith from the same dust. And on their first night in the garden, Adam mounts her to have sex with her. Then she says 'Get off me. Why should you lie on top of me in the superior position when we were made at the same time, from the same stuff?' He rapes her. She cries out in God's name, is drawn up into the stratosphere, and then enjoys a subsequent career as the stereotypical she-demon, responsible for stillbirths on the one hand, and wet dreams on the other. She thereby becomes an emblem of that which most destabilises the traditional images of women (stillbirths) and traditional images of men (wet dreams, when the man loses control of his sexuality). But I do not want to focus on Lilith herself. What I want to underline is the idea that this version of the first couple's story shows how politicised the primal scene is. Not Adam and Eve and seduction, but Adam and Lilith and the dominant/submissive politics of marital rape. So, when people ask 'Had Diana got too powerful?' it may be to the revolutionary Lilith or primal scene dimension that they are referring. This forms the mythopoetic background to the conspiracy theories of the causes of Diana's death: she had to be stopped.

For individuals, I suggest that the imagery they have at this moment of their parents' intimate life and sexual relationship is an extremely useful indicator of their politicality – meaning their political values, desire and capacity to do politics. The primal scene moves between conflict and harmony, harmony and conflict. In particular, isn't it about enjoying enough conflict, enough sense of vigourous in-and-out movement, to achieve a harmonious result such as mutual sexual satisfaction, or a baby? The imagery people have in their hearts and in their mind's eye of their parents' sexual relationship tells them a lot about their political selfhood, provided they decode it that way. It can be a self-administered diagnostic test of one's political potential to handle conflict creatively. (For a more detailed account of this way of thinking, see Samuels, 1994, pp. 167–70).

Continuing to explore the latent politics of the Diana phenomenon, I suggest that, particularly towards the end of her life, Diana emerged as a new kind of leader. As such, she forced many of us to question, yet again, whether current and conventional heroic models of leadership are adequate for the age in which we live. The top-down model of leadership is one-sided and patriarchal and wastes the imaginative political energy that is certainly available in the populace for a bottom-up approach. So we end up with a demoralised people and a power-hungry elite. Diana became the visible aspect of long-standing alternative ideas about leadership, which had been dubbed 'feminine' or 'maternal'. (Such ideas have already found their way into hard-boiled management consultancy theory.) The changing of relations between politicians who lead and citizens who are led is on any thoughtful contemporary political agenda, and the Diana phenomenon may be understood as part of this move.

My second question concerned how moods transmit in our culture. Literal answers would highlight the role of the media, and simple explanations, such as that people speak to each other. Whilst these answers are not wrong, they offer only an incomplete explanation. The media operates all the time and people speak all the time and we do not experience such discernable collective moods every time that something happens. The question about how *Zeitgeists* form remains open.

Psychoanalysis has an answer: at an incredibly rapid rate, introjections and projections take place and a mood or something shared arises out of these ins-and-outs between people. This theory is also satisfactory as far as it goes, but does not take account of the fact that there is also a 'primary togetherness' in large groups, societies and nations. Psychoanalysis – as opposed to Jungian psychology – assumes a 'primary separateness' which we struggle to bridge with our projections and introjections. Psychoanalysis is today's principal inheritor of the Western idea of the autonomous separate ego, which it not only sees as the beginning state, but valorises as a desirable goal. In the Jungian view, though some accounts of the process of individuation may seem to praise separateness, the overall thrust involves the individual rejoining the collective (Jung, 1934, par. 275). However, Jungian theory does not fully explain *Zeitgeists* either. I do not think we can put the reaction to Diana's death down to the existence of a collective unconscious, or even of a cultural unconscious (Henderson, 1985). We can say that concepts such as these are the best known examples in psychology of a tradition which is totally foreign to psychoanalysis in that they assume primary togetherness rather than primary separation.

For Jung, psyche and matter were, at what he called the psychoid level of the unconscious, two sides of a coin. In my own reworking of his ground-breaking concept of the psychoid, I speak not just of the linkage of psyche and matter, but also of psyche, matter, *and the social* (Samuels, 1994, pp. 72–3). There is a ceaseless shifting and swapping of basal positions. At one, the psychological is more influential, at another the material, at the next, the social.

Many people stated that there was something 'archetypal' about the death of Diana. I believe that if there is anything archetypal about anything at all of which we might speak, it is to be found in the general realm of affects, which seem very nearly universal. It was the shock and sadness that Diana's death produced – that the most famous face and body in the world was no more – that took us into the archetypal area. This was not because she was an 'arche-typal' princess, or an 'archetypal' *belle dame sons merci,* or an 'archetypal' representative of modern woman, but because the emotions engendered in us were of such an impassioned and deep intensity that they threw us into the archetypal realm (see Samuels, 1989, pp. 17–56). The archetypal lives in the beholder or witness, not in the things or people he or she engages with.

Affects and emotions are rooted in the body, and I want now to address the third and last of the promised three issues: to do with the body, sexuality, including 'maternal sexuality', and femininity in society.

Diana's death triggered collective responses to the human body in general and the female body in particular. Her reputation as a person who hugged others, her care for her own beauty, the exercise regimes, the much-reported bulimia and even the nature of the charities to which she seemed particularly drawn – AIDS, leprosy, the landmine campaign – all have to do with and draw us towards the body. There was a permitted sacralisation and valorisa-tion of body here on a scale we have not seen before in post-industrial times. This is significant, because of the way in which the body has been kept down in the Western tradition. Mostly, the body is dumb, it is feminine, stigmatised as housing a temptress, fit to be demeaned and needing to be transcended. Even in our own days, when we cosset it, massage it, adorn it with clothes, take it to the gym, we are still in a very uneasy relationship with it, still trying to control it, to keep it down, to improve it. There is still not much acceptance of the body as it is, and Diana not only shared in that but took corporeal anxiety to new heights. Yet in those images of the Princess using her own perfectly honed body to embrace people whose bodies were maimed, disfigured or wasted, collective acceptance of the human body in its entirety became more visible, more 'official'.

As far as her sexuality was concerned, I do not see Diana as the mere combination of mother and sexual icon which many commentators noted. I see her more as an image of *maternal sexuality,* where the two are already joined. The topic of maternal sexuality is, of course, a highly emotive and taboo-ed one. The French psychoanalyst Jean Laplanche (1976) posits that what inspires psychological growth is the seductiveness of the '(m)other'. By the action of her sexuality, she seduces the growth potential out of the child, who longs to join with her and so must 'move' and grow in order to do so. For Laplanche, this primary seductiveness accounts for the origins of psyche itself, which is , so to speak, drawn out of the individual by something sexual. Diana certainly drew out our psyches and this is why it is reasonable to see her not as simply 'mother plus sex', but as an image of maternal sexuality itself. When this topic is discussed, the 'seductive mother' is often seen as a bad one in the professional literature. Yet, according to Laplanche, without her seduction of the child, there would be no psychic activity or growth. If his analysis is in any way pertinent, then Diana's life and death are good examples of the primary seduction of maternal sexuality and it was we, the public, who were (healthily) seduced. The public mood at the time of her death contained all the energy you would expect to see when it is drawn out by this kind of seduction, which I would see as carried by the maternal body. Diana's maternal sexuality quite literally drew the potential out of people.

In this short piece, I have tried not only to deal with psychological and political aspects of the death of Diana, but also to make some constructive use of the reactions to her death as stimulus to fresh thought at the interface of psychology and politics. Isn't this one of the most widespread responses to her death: a rethink about what happens at the places where personal and political, private and public, internal and external, meet? From these liminal perspectives, Diana may be understood as inspiring and symbolising a change in the way we think about ourselves and our societies – as well as standing as a necessary, disillusioning brake on too much optimism about either the world or ourselves.

REFERENCES

Freud, S. (1920). 'Post-scriptum to a discussion on lay analysis', *SE* 20: 235ff. London: Hogarth Press.

Henderson, J. (1985). *Cultural Attitudes in Perspective*. Toronto: Inner City Books.

Jung, C. G. (1934). 'The relations between the ego and the unconscious'. *CW* 7: 121-239. London: Routledge & Kegan Paul, 1953.

Jung, C. G. (1946). 'Preface to "Essays on Contemporary Events"'. *CW* 10: 177. London: Routledge & Kegan Paul, 1974.

Laplanche, J. (1976). *Life and Death in Analysis*. Baltimore: Johns Hopkins.

Orbach, S. (1998). 'Beyond the grand emotions: the value of disappointment', unpublished lecture.

Samuels, A. (1989). *The Plural Psyche*. London and New York: Routledge.

Samuels, A. (1994). *The Political Psyche*. London and New York: Routledge.

Stanton, M. (1992). Personal communication.

Sacred and Profane Paradoxes of Monarchy

ANN CASEMENT

As the whole world now knows, Diana, Princess of Wales, was elevated to royal status after her marriage to Prince Charles and subsequently deprived of it after their divorce. This essay is a circumnambulation of the term royal, in its application both to the 'Royal Family' and to the Princess of Wales. This narrower focus will be inter-related with the wider implications of the 'divine' when it is associated with monarchy. The twin lenses of Jungian psychology and social anthropology will be the instruments of this exploration, interspersed with occasional visits to *The Golden Bough*.

Jung differentiates collective consciousness from collective unconsciousness in the following manner: 'Ego-consciousness seems to be dependent on two factors: firstly, on the conditions of the collective, i.e. the social, conscious; and secondly, on the archetypes, or dominants, of the collective unconsciousness.' (Jung, 1954, par. 423). The former is the repository of the social, philosophical, ethical and religious problems of any one time; the latter, in contrast, is timeless and is the realm of archetypal and instinctual contents – archetypes being the inherited structuring patterns of the psyche that are linked to instinct. Royalty in its secular and divine aspects transcends collective consciousness and unconsciousness, having its two halves firmly rooted in each of these realms. It is this aspect of royalty – the duality of sacred and profane – that is the main focus here.

Symbols emanate from the collective unconscious whereas signs come from the collective conscious. 'Those conscious contents which give us a clue to the unconscious background are incorrectly called *symbols* by Freud', says

Jung (Jung, 1966, par. 105). 'They are not true symbols however, since according to his theory they have merely the role of *signs* or *symptoms* of the subliminal process. The true symbol differs essentially from this and should be understood as an expression of an intuitive idea that cannot yet be formulated in any other or better way'.

The death of Diana represented equally symbol and sign. For many, it was shrugged off as the product of media manipulation and mass hysteria; for others, it had the effect of the symbol in mystifying and unifying large numbers of people. The impact of the symbol derives from its *numinosity*, which Jung defines as 'a quality belonging to a visible object or the influence of an invisible presence that causes a peculiar alteration of consciousness' (Jung, 1940, par. 6).

A numinous experience has the full force of a confrontation with something that is as yet undisclosed but which is experienced as fateful and meaningful. This kind of feeling often acts as a catalyst for unifying people on a collective level and leads to an experience of liminality and community. Victor Turner, that most Jungian of anthropologists, talks of liminality as blending 'lowliness and sacredness, homogeneity and comradeship' (Turner, 1995, p. 96). Community, or *communitas*, the Latin version that he prefers, describes 'society as an unstructured or rudimentarily structured and relatively undifferentiated . . . community, or even communion of equal individuals who submit together to the general authority of the ritual elders' (ibid).

Shortly after Diana's death, *The Economist* had a leader expressing its collective feeling of being mystified at the strength of its own reaction to the event. Here is an extract from a letter I sent in response:

(Re) your . . . overwhelming response to the extraordinary events of last week. What you describe is the mystifying, unifying, healing and changing power of the symbol. The feelings of community that have been engendered . . . are another aspect of the symbol at work.

Given the largely secular bias of *The Economist*, I was very surprised to see my letter published at the top of the letters column. At the same time, it felt like another example of the huge role played by the media in Diana's outer life. Her other more private side sought the solace of different forms of therapy. *Mercurius* – the alchemical name given to Hermes, that many-hued and wily deity – is the patron god of both communication and therapy and it is in this Janus-like dual aspect which is always associated with that particular deity that we experience the two sides of Diana.

A brief description of both Mercurius and Janus would seem appropriate at this point. The dual nature of what Jung calls the Trickster is a reflection of Mercurius – half animal/half divine, a seemingly negative figure that yet manages to achieve through stupidity what others fail to achieve through wit or straightforward cleverness. The Trickster is compensatory to consciously held views and goals and manifests through slips of the tongue, accidents and coincidences. Above all, in its power to bring transformation through new energy, it has the numinosity of all saviour-like figures.

The Roman god, Janus, was the animistic spirit that guarded doorways (*januae*) and archways (*jani*). His symbol is a double-faced head, which depicts his dual nature in being able to face simultaneously both outwards and inwards and he is in this way associated with both outer and inner. In other words, he is the guardian of the liminal place that Turner describes above.

Intriguingly, when I consulted what *The Golden Bough* has to say about the goddess Diana, I discovered that Frazer makes the link between her and the goddess Jana, the spouse of Janus. Both Jana and Diana were goddesses of fecundity and childbirth and identified with the moon, which is also the ruling planet of the Princess of Wales' birth sign of Cancer.

Janus-like, Princess Diana presented her outer Cancerian carapace of glamour to the media. The inner world of pain that was betrayed by those large sad eyes she took to therapy. As stated above, both disciplines share the ruling deity of Mercurius but towards each he presents a different aspect. In his aspect of messenger, Mercurius is god of the media, who infects journalists with an insatiable desire to find out secrets in order to be able to tell about them. In his aspect of psychopomp, he is the figure who guides the psyche at times of transition and liminality and it is this aspect of Mercurius/ Hermes which is the god of therapy. In the course of therapy, this figure may be seen to be embodied by the therapist, which bestows on him or her the privilege of being the repository of secrets combined with the responsibility of being able to hold and contain them.

Let us return briefly to the theme of the Trickster as it plays an important part in the approach this chapter takes to Diana. It embodies compensatory energy both to the conscious attitude of the individual and also for the collective. In other words, it points the way to what Jung calls *shadow* – all which is denied and rejected because seen as inferior on a personal and collective level. Shadow is an archetype and as such brings with it powerful affect when it is constellated, particularly on a collective level. Once again, we are confronted with the duality of opposites, in this instance the duality of light equated with consciousness and ego and dark equated with shadow. The opposites incorporated in Mercurius are each other's shadow and it is these opposites that are to be found in, on the one hand, the media and, on the other, therapy. This may go some way to explaining the uneasy relationship that exists between the two – the media, for instance, indulging in endless envious attacks on therapy and therapists; the latter, for their part, seemingly frozen into a state of paranoid projection onto the media.

Duality is a constant theme in association with Diana, another example of it being the saint/whore projections she attracted onto herself. This image of the sacred prostitute belongs to the pagan world before it was split into Mary and Magdalen by Christianity. It recurs in alchemical texts as the chaste bride and whore combined in the chaos of undifferentiated matter wherein lies the hidden deity (Mercurius) that contains the potential new life. This will be elaborated below in the section on the alchemical incestuous union.

In life, Diana was often scapegoated as well as adulated and she carried the sins of the many. So her death may be seen as a ritual sacrifice. The scapegoat performs for society that most cohesive function of all: providing a dustbin for the collective shadow. The redeemer is above all a scapegoat and by his or her sacrifice a ritual act of catharsis or purging society of all its impurities takes place. After the rite of sacrifice comes the rite of incorporation, which here was collectively acted-out by the devouring of anything about Diana in the media. This act of incorporation both takes in and potentially integrates the energy of the saviour and also helps salve the conscience of all concerned in the scapegoating and subsequent sacrifice. In this way, social glue is restored.

The awe with which the archetype of Death grips us all and its place in the scheme of things is well-understood by both Jung and Durkheim. For Jung, death and rebirth are two sides of the same archetype or psychic reality at work in an individual – and in the collective – throughout life. When individual ego-consciousness and the social ego are confronted by a numinous event or image, the result may be a defeat of the ego which is experienced as a death. In this death lies the potential new life which, incorporated, can lead to a further expansion of the ego. This has been touched on in the paragraph above on incorporation and will be elaborated in the section below on alchemy.

For Durkheim, society and the social order was the focus of attention and he was always fascinated by anything that added to social glue: to paraphrase Jung, one might say that for Durkheim, Society was a numinosum. According to him, funeral or mourning rites were in a special category of their own. He named these piacular or expiatory rites, where sadness and sorrow are the dominant emotions. Rites of mourning produce a veritable 'panic of sorrow', the social function of which is to draw the group together when its solidarity is threatened by the loss of an individual. In this way, the group reaffirms its permanence in the face of the transience of the individual.

For Durkheim, all ritual in one way or another is there to shore up social cohesion. Religious ceremonial is the culmination, bringing together members of a society in an act of self-worship, the ultimate in social glue. So, in ritually sanctifying and worshipping Diana, people were ultimately taking part in their own sanctification.

In *The Elementary Forms of the Religious Life*, Durkheim's central thesis is that there are no religions which are false.

Religious beliefs and practices undoubtedly seem disconcerting at times, and one is tempted to attribute them to some sort of a deep-seated error. But one must know how to go underneath the symbol to the reality which it represents and which gives it its meaning (Durkheim, 1965, p. 14).

Durkheim of course means 'social reality' where Jung would substitute 'psychic reality'. But apart from that the two would probably be in agreement with the rest of the statement. Ultimately for Durkheim, the sacred referred to those things in society that were forbidden or set apart; and since this came about through an act by society, he concluded that the sacred force must be society itself.

Through a variety of acts sanctioned by British society in which they were embedded, Diana had royal/divine status conferred upon and later taken from her. Through marriage to a royal prince she was invested with the title 'royal' but divested of it through divorce. However, this was a 'royal' who had a deep intuitive understanding of the duality of the sacred and profane body of the monarchy and her life became increasingly one of privilege combined with an extraordinary empathy with the under-privileged. Her common touch, both literal and figurative, can also be seen as an antidote to the King's Evil, an illness which only the monarch's touch can cure.

The term King's Evil was originally the rather fanciful name for scrofula, a tubercular swelling of the lymph glands that was popularly believed to be curable by the touch of royalty. Versions of this belief can be found at different times in other societies, but in England the custom was first adopted in the reign of Edward the Confessor. It reached its zenith at the time of the Restoration when Charles II was said to have touched more than 90,000 people. The last royal healer in England was Queen Anne. The custom then dwindled out of existence until it was revived in recent years by Diana.

It is interesting to speculate why this phenomenon takes on new life at certain times. Charles II was restored to the throne with the monarchial powers claimed by his father somewhat modified and had to demonstrate that he was fully aware of both the profane and the sacred aspects of the monarch. Being literally 'in touch' with the common people would have been a way of demonstrating this duality. Diana seems to have been what Jung would call a 'feeling' type – someone who has an intuitive feel for the emotional needs of other individuals or of the collective. Out of her own suffering she was brought into touch with that of millions of others. In this way and in her own right she gradually assumed the mantle of divine and profane royalty. Diana's 'touch', in both its literal and metaphorical senses, contrasts with the actual monarch's seemingly being 'out of touch' with the sentiments of the people. This was a point that was made, often forcibly, by the media at the time of Diana's death.

In the symbolic form of Diana, the duality of the sacred and profane aspects of monarchy were seen to coalesce. It would be well to explore this dichotomy of the sacred and the profane and their internal interrelationship before going on to further exploration of the concept of sacred kingship.

A person or thing was designated as sacred when it was unique or extraordinary. Closely related to the Latin *sacer* is the word *numen* which means 'mysterious power' or 'god'. The term numinous was introduced in 1917 by Rudolf Otto in his seminal work which was translated into English as *The Idea of the Holy* in 1923. Since then it has been used as a description of the sacred as the power before which humankind trembles. Correlates of *sacer* include the Greek *hagios*, Hebrew *qadosh*, Polynesian *tapu*, and Arabic *haram*; correlates of *numen* include the Melanesian *mana*, the Sioux *wakanda*, the old German *haminja*, and Sanskrit *Brahman*.

The sacred is separated from the common (profane) world and appears in myths, sounds, ritual activity, people, and natural objects, which may come together to confer sacred status on an object, be it a person or an activity. Through the retelling of a myth the divine action that was done 'in the beginning' is repeated. The repetition of the sacred action symbolically duplicates the power that originally established the world. The recognition of sacred power in the myth and ritual is related to the notion of sound, for instance, the name of a god or an arbitrary sound like the Hindu *om*, or the Judaic/Christian *hallelujah*.

The sacred thus expresses the ultimate total value and meaning of life. It is the eternal reality, which is recognized to have been before it was known and to be known differently from the way in which common things are known, through myth or ritual activity. However, the duality of sacred/profane is further complicated by the fact that the sacred could itself include the dichotomy pure/unpure. For instance, the Polynesian *tapu* designates something as not 'free' for common use because of its extraordinary energy, which includes both generating and polluting forces.

Anyone unprotected by special powers who comes into contact with the sacred could be polluted and destroyed by it as it was restricted to divine use only. Incest, for example, is a prerogative of the gods and not allowed to ordinary mortals – a theme which will be explored more fully later. Only a person who had entered the divine realm was pure and this transition was often marked by a ritual act of rebirth. The concept of the twice-born in India and Jung's alchemical model of death and rebirth are examples which point to the actual material birth of an individual and to a subsequent symbolic rebirth.

There is a further ambiguity. What one person regards as sacred or profane may not necessarily be so regarded by others. In other words, what is sacred for some is profane for others. This goes a long way in explaining the conflicting responses to what has come to be known as the 'Diana phenomenon'. Otto elaborated his understanding of the sacred from this basic ambiguity. The sacred sets the boundary of human limitation but it also represents the unlimited possibility that draws us beyond the limiting spatio-temporal structures of human existence. Only the sacred can fulfill humankind's deepest needs, thus the reverence shown to the sacred is composed of both trust and terror.

The concept of sacred kingship has been a preoccupation since ancient times. This is related to what Jung calls the 'Self' which is for him the central and unifying principle of the whole psyche, both consciousness and the unconscious. Seen in this way, the Self is no less than another image of the divine and often manifests in dreams or phantasies as a royal personage.

On the level of outer reality, the sacred ruler was the possessor of supernatural powers, both beneficent and malevolent. In former times, power resided in one person who had the necessary physical and psychic strength over both people and objects. The king's power extended over everything within his community and only gradually was this power shared with others within the community. A residual belief from this era is that collective mores and national feelings of self-worth are still felt to derive from the transcendent position of the monarch. In Britain, for instance, the primacy of family life and values are felt to be encapsulated in the institution of the 'Royal Family'. If marriage and family life amongst the royals are seen to be problematic, this in turn engenders a degree of permissiveness amongst ordinary families.

Much of Frazer's *The Golden Bough* is concentrated on the study of divine kingship and power and of how different societies deal with its loss in their ruler. In his chapter on the killing of the divine king – a widespread motif – Frazer devotes considerable space to C. G. Seligman's ethnological account of the Shilluk, a Nilotic people who inhabit the southern part of the Sudan and who numbered about 110,000 in the 1970s. In 1909 when Seligman visited them, they were united in a single tribal state headed by a divine king to whom great reverence was paid, as he was thought to derive his power from the spirit of the semi-divine hero who founded the royal dynasty. Frazer gives a particularly colourful account of how the Shilluk went about their regular custom of putting the king to death whenever he showed signs of ill-health or failing strength.

For this tribal people, failing strength was directly equated with failing potency and when the king showed an incapacity to satisfy the sexual passions of his wives (of whom he had a great many) the latter would report this to the chiefs. They would intimate the bad news of his impending doom to the king by spreading a white cloth over his face and knees as he lay slumbering in the heat of the sultry afternoon. Execution soon followed sentence of death in a hut, specially built for the occasion, into which the king was led and where he lay down with his head resting on the lap of a nubile virgin. The hut was then walled up and the two were left to perish of starvation and suffocation. This long drawn out process was later ameliorated and the king was despatched more quickly by being strangled in a hut specially built for the occasion.

The custom of putting the divine king to death at the first sign of his failing power is the Shilluk way of preserving the divine spirit by which he is animated 'in the most perfect state of efficiency' (Frazer, 1971, p. 353). Putting the king to death while he is still vigorous and physically attractive ensures that this divine spirit is transmitted to his successor whilst it is still unimpaired by weakness or old age.

Youth, vigour and sexual attraction are thus all necessary attributes of divine kingship. This was evidenced after Diana's death by the debate about the monarchy and the succession. It may be that her death while still in full youth and vigour fulfilled the archetypal role of ensuring the continuing potency of the monarchy. It also served to draw attention to the ageing Queen and Prince Charles, which is a possible explanation for the populist idea that the latter should be passed over in favour of the (young) Prince William. Overnight it seemed that the great archetype of Death had conferred divine status on Diana, which combined with the divine status projected onto her by 'the people', arising as it seemed spontaneously from the grass roots. The monarch was seen to be out of favour because she was too remote, and further had, in what appeared as a petty act of vengeance, removed Diana's royal status. Even the legitimacy of this act was questioned. Hence the monarch lost, at least temporarily, her status, which was now seen by many to reside instead in Diana and her immediate heirs, her two sons.

So the death of Diana has been a catalyst in focusing attention on reforming an institution which the British hold dear but which has, at the same time, become perceived as aloof and distant from ordinary people. The movement for reform of a monarchy that has been set in aspic for the whole of this century is now seen to reside with Tony Blair, 'the people's' spokesman and one might almost say, high priest, who played such a significant role in enabling the transition of Diana to 'the people's princess'.

Let us see if we can elaborate further what this latter term means, if anything. Ritual sacrifice of Diana as scapegoat-saviour leads to purification and to her to coming to life in a different form – in other words to ritual rebirth. Death, both symbolic and actual, is the great archetypal transformer of an individual's status from that of profane to that of sacred. (Again, reference to Jung's alchemical analogy is appropriate here.) Death purified Diana of her mis-doings and sufferings and in one great cathartic event transformed her into a divine being. Identification with her as a saviour figure dying for their sins holds out hope for millions of other suffering, venal human beings that they too can experience this kind of salvation. In a 'panic of sorrow' on the part of millions of people, a new icon is born out of mass projection and once again we see society worshipping itself by way of worshipping the icon. In this way, society itself can be seen to be divine and to confer divine status on the object of its reverence. As a result, social glue is reinforced, instilling sentiments of *communitas* and, for a while, the feelings of degeneration that have been around as we approach the millenium are swept away in a great act of renewal and regeneration. In embodying simultaneously divinity, royalty and humanity in the one person, Diana has managed to fulfill all the criteria that make for a focal point for collective identification.

What we witnessed on a collective level in the extraordinary events of the summer of 1997 was a panic of sorrow. I would like to try to link this collective process to individual process in the course of a long Jungian analysis.

A great part of the analytic process is taken up with mourning the loss of the past which entails leaving behind childhood and the whole of the first half of life in order to start on the path of individuating, beginning to realize one's own potential. Just as for an individual in analysis, private emotions are connected to the greater realm of the collective unconscious, so for huge numbers of people after the death of Diana, private emotions publicly expressed connected personal experience to a wider feeling of being part of a group process, *communitas*. As Durkheim says of piacular rites: 'Eventually one stops mourning, and one does so because of the mourning itself' (Durkheim, 1965, p. 448). This represents the stage of rebirth into a new order – both for the individual and for the collective.

It was in his discovery of alchemy that Jung at last found the link which connected the past with his analytical approach. The most impressive example of this is *The Psychology of the Transference*, in which Jung undertook the analysis of a series of alchemical pictures from the sixteenth-century *Rosarium philosophorum*. Through analysing the incestuous longings between the King and Queen depicted by the left-handed contact between them in an early picture, Jung extrapolates the experience of erotic and incestuous longings in any long-term analysis. The incestuous element evident in the *Rosarium* between the betrothed couple is symbolised in several of the pictures by the brother-sister relationship of Apollo and Diana or Sol and Luna. In the second picture, a dove descending between the incestuous pair with a rose in its beak unites their crossed roses and points to the spiritual or divine love awakening between them. The next two pictures show that the left-handed relationship is no more and the two hands of each are connected by the uniting symbol of the flowers.

So if incestuous feelings can be contained and not acted-out in an analysis – what Jung means by the *opus contra naturam* – the incestuous libido may be transformed into spiritual libido and both analyst and analysand participate in a higher or royal marriage that leaves both more fully integrated and evolved as personalities. Along the way, both are exposed to experiences of death and depression but eventual rebirth may take place through the constellation of the symbol of the divine child which represents new life. Herein lies the true import of the analytic relationship.

I would like to try to relate the alchemical relationship depicted in the *Rosarium* to the psychologically incestuous union of Diana and her brother, Charles Spencer – emphasising that what is being talked about here is symbolic incest and *not* actual physical incest. If incest, or 'kinship libido' as Jung calls it, can be internalized and in this way spiritualized rather than lived sexually, it then has the possibility of activating the spirituality that is potentially there in everyone and of bringing rebirth and new life. This is the deeper significance of the symbolic incestuous union to the collective experience.

The crowning moment of the funeral service was Spencer's eulogy, which contained some of the following words and phrases: symbol, compassion, transcended, joy, soul, God-given, goddess, anguish, love. How Jungian! Most moving of all was when he talked of his sister's 'innermost feelings of suffering that made it possible for her to connect with her constituency of the rejected'. One of the valuable things I learned from the pain engendered through the voyage of self-discovery that epitomizes Jungian analysis was exactly what Spencer had managed to convey in those poignant few words. What this means is a confrontation with the *shadow* which affords the possibility of a rehabilitation of all the inferior, weak and despised parts of oneself. This experience leads to an ability to be open to the rejected parts of others.

There were two targets for Spencer's anger in the address, the first being the media. The second was less direct, but one could hardly escape the obvious meaning in the following words about the Princess's two sons.

We will not allow them to suffer the anguish that used regularly to drive you to tearful despair. And beyond that . . . I pledge that we, your blood family, will do all we can to continue the imaginative and loving way in which you were steering these two exceptional young men so that their souls are not simply immersed by duty and tradition but can sing openly as you planned.

This is the voice of the brother/lover reclaiming the children of this psychological incestuous union with his sister/lover. Let us remind ourselves that incest is the prerogative of the divine and of royalty and this symbolic incestuous union, this *hierosgamos* as Jung terms it, touched and moved the world's soul.

Diana's death, like her life, has been a catalyst for the Royal Family and has already brought about change which looks likely to continue. While she was alive, there were claims that her affair with Dodi Fayed was a source of embarrassment to the establishment; she presumably had some inkling of this. Yet her death has put royalty back in the space it has to inhabit between the sacred and profane if it is to be both a living symbol and also in touch with people's actual life experience. Once again we are brought face-to-face with the mercurial transformative quality that was so central to Diana's way of being. She possessed, and was possessed by, a quality that must be extraordinarily uncomfortable for the individual on whom Mercurius bestows it: like him, they have the quality of being all things to all people. I have talked to innumerable people since her death – family, friends, colleagues, patients, analysands, acquaintances – and each has a quite definitive view of Diana.

She was, in the end, someone who attracted every kind of projection. And that, perhaps, is what is involved in the making of an icon – the very word being a derivative of the Greek *eikon*, meaning image.

Myths and alchemy provide maps for psychological development and insight and it is particularly at times when there is a collective 'panic of sorrow' that we turn to them for help and enlightenment. Alchemy was seen as heretical in medieval times because its lively imagery differed from an increasingly sexless Christianity, just as psychoanalysis later differed from Victorian rationalism and suppression. Jung called alchemy 'a grand projected image of unconscious thought processes' (Jaffé, 1979, p. 97), and was drawn to it because it represented a shift away from concretism to the capacity for symbolization and creative fantasy. Above all, it represented communion with a highly ambivalent god, base and impish on the one hand and divine on the other. It has been the main thrust of this essay to point to this ambivalent deity as the ruler of the life and ultimate destiny of Diana, Princess of Wales.

REFERENCES

Durkheim E. (1965). *The Elementary Forms of the Religious Life: A Study in Religious Sociology*, trans. Joseph Ward Swain. London: Allen & Unwin/New York: Macmillan.
Frazer J. (1971). *The Golden Bough: A Study in Magic and Religion*. London: Macmillan.
Jaffé, A. (1979). *C. G. Jung: Word and Image*. Princeton: Princeton University Press.
Jung, C. G. (1940). 'Psychology and Religion', *CW*, 11: 3–105. London: Routledge & Kegan Paul, 1958.
— (1954). 'On the Nature of the Psyche'. *CW*, 8: 159–234. London: Routledge & Kegan Paul, 1960.
— (1934). 'On the Relation of Analytical Psychology to Poetry', *CW*, 15: 65–83. London: Routledge & Kegan Paul, 1966.
Turner, V. (1995). *The Ritual Process*. New York: Walter de Gruyter.

Collective Masks of Individuality and Virtual Spirituality

RENOS K. PAPADOPOULOS

'FOREVER YOUNG, FOREVER LOVED'

These were the words the British newspaper *News of the World* had on the cover of a special pull-out section on Princess Diana, on 18 January 1998. Nobody is, of course, 'forever young' or 'forever loved'; even mythical figures that remain seemingly unchanged by time are subject to changes, at least in people's perceptions and according to the prevailing *Zeitgeist*. The preposterous suggestion that somebody could possibly remain associated forever with youth and love can only be understood in the context of a special and powerful mythology, not just any ordinary mythology. But, as we know, Princess Diana was not just any ordinary person; she was a very special international figure; she was, indeed, a star. It is not possible for just any-body to be a star; stars, after all, have no bodies as such. Their bodies are not made of ordinary human and mortal stuff but of dream stuff.

Princess Diana was not just a star but a super-star and a mega-star. One of the characteristics of actual physical stars, as opposed to planets, is that they are fixed and they do not shift positions. The word planet comes from a verb which in its active form, *plano*, means 'to lead astray' and in its passive form, *planoumai*, means 'to wander'. So, planets are wandering bodies which can be led astray, in a sense, by other heavenly bodies, the stars. Another characteristic of planets is that they do not have their own light, whereas stars do. Thus, stars are self-sufficient and independent entities in so far as they shine from within and do not follow anybody else's orbit.

It must have been these attributes of stars, in addition to their distant, mysterious and magic qualities, that have prompted people to describe certain celebrities as 'stars'. Contrary to common perception, the word 'star' is not a modern expression and it was not coined by the media; it has been used with this meaning as far back as the 'golden age' of classical Greece and Euripides, in his tragedy *Hippolitus*, may have been the first to use it. *The Oxford English Dictionary* defines this kind of star as 'a person of brilliant reputation or talents, one who "shines" in society'. The etymology of the English word 'star' comes from a very old root with similar words in most ancient languages: in Greek it is *aster* or *astron*, in Sanskrit *staras* or *tara*, in Gothic *stairno*, and most modern European languages use derivatives from this root. However, an etymological exploration reveals an interesting twist. In Greek, *aster* is related to (a) *teirea*, which (always plural) is translated as 'the heavenly constellations, signs' (Liddell and Scott, 1869, p. 1609) and to (b) *teras* which is 'a sign, wonder, marvel, of any appearance or event, in which men believed that they could see the finger of God, and read the future'; hence, *teras* also refers to 'anything that serves as a divine sign or omen; as a huge, unearthly creature, a monster' (ibid, p. 1617). Both *teirea* and *teras* are related to the verb *teiro* 'to rub, rub away: of the effects of pain, sorrow etc. on body and mind' but also 'to wear away, wear out, distress, afflict', and in its passive form, 'to suffer', 'to be distressed'. This is the root of 'trauma', as well.

The etymological connections confirm what is usually felt about celebrity stars: as well as the glitter and glamour there is often something ominous, even dark about them. They may not all have teratomorphic characteristics but they are likely to have traumatic histories. However, the etymological probe reveals that the verb *teiro* refers to distress and trauma as well as healing and rubbing away the effects of pain and anguish. In other words, in addition to their external twinkling grandeur, stars could be the agents of both distress and healing. This means that stardom may bring about traumatic suffering and/or liberating healing to the star himself or herself, their friends and family, and even to the wider circle of admirers. The radiating shine from stars with its potential healing or distressing capacity cannot be limited to a small circle; the unearthly light is transmitted from afar (light-years away, so to speak), affecting the widest possible variety of people.

Princess Diana's personality combined some striking opposites which placed her in a special and most attractive category of stars. Her sparkling disposition had a sense of tragedy about it, her splendor was closely associated with disarming simplicity, and her joy was almost visibly linked with her pain. Far from being a self-sufficient and immovable star, she was a most vulnerable and shaky person; although she shone her own light, she was strongly swayed by other people's orbits, and despite her ethereal quality, she inhabited a body which displayed both her charms and her afflictions. Finally, her very mortality tragically confirmed that she was a human star indeed.

This is what makes a star even more attractive: when stardom is paradoxically combined with its opposite, its humanness. Princess Diana was not an immovable star but a most *moving* one, in more than one sense: she was an insecure and wobbly person who kept doing moving things, she did not hide it whenever she was herself moved, she moved people and there was something very moving about her. In this way, it could be said that she combined star qualities with planet characteristics. Despite her social stability in a well established position, emotionally she was very much a 'wanderer' and she was 'led astray' on many occasions. She was a 'flawed' star and this brought her closer to the people, who loved the idea that a star could also be so near to them. The perception that she was not a distant and unearthly star but a human and most moving one set the scene so that after her death she could pass into the realm beyond time and the fluctuations of human emotions and become 'forever young' and 'forever loved'.

How are we to understand the contradictions she embodied and the incredibly powerful fascination they exerted? In so far as the key constituting elements of this phenomenon involve both the personal and collective realms, it would be appropriate to proceed by addressing their interaction. If we were to follow the usual analytic procedures and turn our searchlight exclusively on Princess Diana's individual life and history, we would miss the important interplay between these two domains.

PERSONA AND INDIVIDUATION

During her life and since her death, people have been talking about the 'Princess Diana Phenomenon', in addition to referring to her own person. This means that apart from the person there is an actual 'phenomenon' which, of course, interconnects with the personal reality whilst, at the same time, being also independent of it. It is difficult to delineate precisely where the 'person' ends and the 'phenomenon' begins and to a certain degree, this overlap occurs with everybody, not only with stars. All of us have aspects of our personality which are predominantly personal or collective, and at different times during the course of life there is a selective emphasis on some of these aspects. Our identity is a unique matrix consisting of the idiosyncrasies of personal traits and history, within the context of collective schemata (Papadopoulos, 1997; Papadopoulos and Hildebrand, 1997). Under ordinary circumstances, this matrix develops in natural ways as the personality unfolds and individual identity keeps being constructed in the interaction with societal and cultural structures. However, for stars, there is a particularly perilous process which may interfere with this natural development. Before focusing on these specific difficulties, it may be useful to examine some of the general dangers inherent in this process and, more specifically, on Jung's approach to the dynamics of this interaction.

Jung made it clear that the process of individuation 'is in the first place a purely natural process, which may in some cases pursue its course without the knowledge or assistance of the individual, and can sometimes forcibly accomplish itself in the face of opposition' (1943, par. 186). Moreover, in so far as individuation 'aims at a living co-operation of all [collective and individual] factors' (Jung, 1928, par. 268), there is a natural process according to which the collective and personal aspects of our identity interweave to create the unique tapestry of our specific individuality.

One of the most important facets of the process of development in every individual is the appropriate negotiation which brings about a working balance and 'co-operation' between the collective and personal dimensions. Jung attributed a crucial role to the 'persona' in relation to this facet. According to him, the persona is an 'arbitrary segment of collective psyche . . . [and] as its name implies, [it is] only a mask of the collective psyche, a mask that feigns individuality, making others and oneself believe that one is individual, whereas one is simply acting a role through which the collective psyche speaks' (ibid, par. 245). Jung clarifies that 'fundamentally, the persona is nothing real: it is a compromise between individual and society as to what a man should appear to be. He takes a name, earns a title, exercises a function, he is this or that. In a certain sense all this is real, yet in relation to the essential individuality of the person concerned it is only a secondary reality, a compromise formation in the making which others often have a greater share in than he' (ibid, par. 246). Consequently, individuals need to have an agency (the persona) that shapes them as separate beings with their own distinct identity and which relates to the outside world. However, in so far as every person has this agency, the persona in itself is a collective, not a personal structure.

Thus, seen from this perspective, individuation implies a central paradox: what is considered uniquely personal is at the same time most collective. Jung expressed it as follows: 'If we endeavour to draw a precise distinction between what psychic material should be considered personal, and what impersonal, we soon find ourselves in the greatest dilemma, for by definition

we have to say of the persona's contents what we have said of the impersonal unconscious, namely, that it is collective' (ibid, par. 245). Hence, in so far
as the persona 'is exclusively concerned with the relation to objects' (Jung,
1921, par. 801), it can serve the useful function of mediating between the individual and the external world. At the same time, the persona may also create
serious problems if this fine distinction among the various realities it
embraces is not maintained.

Jung identifies two ways in which this may happen: the first is a 'regressive
restoration of the persona' (Jung, 1928, par. 254) and the second is
'identification with the collective psyche' (ibid, par. 260). According to the
first, when 'the unconscious contents break through into consciousness' as a
result of a critical event or experience, the individual may react by pretend-
ing to ignore them in order to avoid the conflict they introduce. What the
individual, in effect, then does, 'as a result of his fright', is to '[slip] back to an
earlier phase of his personality' (ibid, par. 254). This is what Jung calls
'regressive restoration of the persona' because the persona comes to the res-
cue of the individual by restoring a previous 'identity' according to which the
current conflict does not exist. In the case of the second, when the individual
cannot cope with the intensity of a newly created conflict, the persona may
identify with the collective psyche. In so far as Jung repeatedly emphasised
that 'access to the collective psyche means a renewal of life for the individual,
no matter whether this renewal is felt as pleasant or unpleasant' (ibid, par.
260), a tremendous power is released when the persona sinks into the collective realm, regardless of the circumstances. The boundarilessness of this
situation may produce healing and renewal. However, this happens at a great
cost: the loss of one's identity. In a poetic way, Jung described this as follows:
'Identification would seem to be the shortest road to this [connection with the
primal source of life], for the dissolution of the persona in the collective
psyche positively invites one to wed oneself with the abyss and blot out all
memory in its embrace' (ibid, par. 260). Both these ways represent failures of
the persona to maintain a balance between the collective and personal realms
and amount to what Jung called 'negative attempts to free the individuality
from the collective psyche' (ibid, par. 254).

Stars are particularly prone to hazardous combinations of these two
dangers. As it is difficult for them regressively to restore their persona in any
visible way, because the sparkle of their stardom cannot allow this to happen,
they may achieve this only in a very private way, which is invisible to others.
What is far easier for them, is to embrace the abyss of the collective psyche.
However, as this could lead to loss of identity, they may attempt to combine

this identification along with a particularly cruel or humiliating regression which is kept outside the public gaze.

COLLECTIVE MASKS OF INDIVIDUALITY

Stars have a unique relation to the collective. All of us, as fathers, mothers, sons, daughters, teachers, students, analysts, analysands, citizens, follow certain prescribed roles which are based on collective prescriptions. Moreover, each day we play several roles depending on where we are and what we do; overall, we manage to switch roles with remarkable ease and dexterity, mostly in an automatic way. The collective dimension is also active in us in many other more subtle ways. Our very sense of identity is a product of the delicate function of the persona which manages to balance the collective and personal aspects of the psyche. However, stars almost by definition are collective entities, their sense of identity depends, to a greater extent, on the collective realm. This makes the process of persona differentiation more hazardous for them.

There are many collective narratives that relate what an individual is, how an individual should behave, how one should become an individual and how one should maintain an individuality. Stars not only adhere to these narratives but, it could be said, actually live them out, incarnate them. The moment one is launched into stardom and acquires star status, it is almost impossible regressively to restore one's persona. The collective nature of stardom cannot possibly allow stars to lower their personas. Even if this were to happen, the public would accept it as a sign of supreme individuality and applaud it, thus transforming it immediately into collective material. This creates a most tragic situation where stars are doomed never to be able to abandon their stardom, regardless of how non-star-like their behaviour becomes. Although this situation is true for most stars, this should not imply that every single star has lost his or her soul. The intensity of this tragic impasse depends on a combination between personal traits and circumstantial, historical and cultural factors.

In trying to connect with the authenticity of her own individuality, Princess Diana desperately attempted to reveal her vulnerabilities: she admitted to adultery, to suffering from eating disorders, even to self-harming behaviour. These revelations had a paradoxically opposite effect: instead of bringing her down from stardom, they made the public love her more, turning her vulnerabilities into charming star characteristics. She tried to withdraw from public life and the public again applauded this move as an excellent piece of stardom (after all, all stars hate being stars and want to be 'individuals'). There was nothing she tried to do in order to connect with her own genuine self which was not owned by the collective; this was so because whatever she did, in fact, fitted perfectly within the collective scenario of what stars do when they try to be individuals.

To be reminded, Jung said that the mask of persona '*feigns individuality*, making others and oneself believe that one is individual, whereas one is simply acting a role through which the collective psyche speaks' (Jung 1928, par. 245). Thus, using similar imagery, it would be apt to say that stars seem to be wearing a 'collective mask of individuality'. By this I mean that the individuality they display may not always be an expression of their unique person but it is likely to be a collective mask which feigns individuality. 'Collective masks of individuality' refer to the sum total of all the narratives that the collective has about how individuals should be and act in order to demonstrate their individuality. This term was first used in the context of a Jungian approach to understanding the phenomenon of another star, Lawrence of Arabia (Papadopoulos, 1990). What I then argued, , was that T. E. Lawrence (1888–1935) was probably the first big hero-star who was created and destroyed by the media and that he failed to connect with his own individuality despite repeated sincere attempts all of which ended up disastrously. In other words, from the moment he assumed stardom and had the 'collective mask of individuality' stuck onto him, no amount of effort could reconnect him with the authenticity of his being.

T. E. Lawrence was a gifted young officer who rose to stardom as a result of fortuitous circumstances. An Oxford scholar who combined shyness with a flamboyant style, a personal woundedness with public outspokenness, Lawrence seems to have been the right person in the right place. When the appalling carnage in the trenches of the western front were the predominant images of the Great War, the refreshing figure of an eccentric Englishman clad in Arab robes fighting the same war but in a different theatre (the Middle East) and against a different enemy (the Turks), was most welcome. The public loved this poet-soldier who was romantically attached to the Arab cause and appeared to be fiercely unconventional (i.e. individual). He was discovered by an American journalist (Lowell Thomas) who created a special show extolling Lawrence's heroic achievements in Arabia. It is estimated that more than four million people saw these live shows (Wilson, 1989, pp. 625–6), a phenomenal number, especially for that time (1918–19). Unable to cope with his enormous popularity, Lawrence attempted, in vain, to withdraw from public exposure and to connect with his own individuality.

Paradoxically, but not uncharacteristically, he tried to achieve this by joining the Army, one of the most collective institutions. The world never stopped being fascinated by him and he was followed everywhere by journalists who kept creating the most incredible stories about him: that he was a Russian spy, that he was to become Hitler's henchman in Britain, etc. When he was killed in a motorcycle accident aged only 47, his death continued the controversies of his life. There were many versions of the events surrounding his death as well as incredible conspiracy theories maintaining that he had been assassinated by agents from at least a dozen different factions ranging from the British, French and Arab intelligence services to anarchists, Zionists, fascists, Bolsheviks, and many others. In other words, in the same way that he did not own his life, he did not even own his death.

What seems to happen to stars is that, tragically, the more they try sincerely to connect with their authenticity, the more they sink back into collective formulae as to how an individual should be. Thus, whereas for ordinary people, the 'negative attempts to free the individuality from the collective psyche' often have a jolting effect which can restore their process of individuation and personal development, for stars this route would be almost inaccessible. Wearing the 'collective mask of individuality', stars cannot possibly follow the 'regressive restoration of the persona' because whatever persona they assume, even a regressed one, the mass of admirers will love it. The more Princess Diana tried to show that she was not a glamorous and independent star with her own light but a broken person with a great deal of suffering, the more the crowd applauded her for being a true star, a star who follows the collective recipe according to which stars despise being stars and yearn to be ordinary people. Following the route of 'identification with the collective psyche' is equally unattainable for stars because they cannot possibly disappear in the collective. Hence, the 'collective mask of individuality' represents a distinct variation of the process of 'identification with the collective psyche' by creating a certain deception, according to which stars, whilst identifying with the collective, still believe that they are only following their own unique and individual path.

Thus, the 'collective mask of individuality' sets stars on a tragic and Sisyphean struggle to gain their individuality; however, the more they strive to achieve this elusive goal, the deeper they sink into enacting collective narratives of how individuals should be. The particular collective persona of a star is void of any personal shadow. Stars have their own constant light; being up in the sky, they are not organised by earthly dimensions, they are not grounded and therefore they cannot possibly have a personal shadow.

Even their shadow is collective. Princess Diana desperately attempted to own her own shadow but she was denied it. No amount of personal blemish could possibly mar her stardom; instead, she carried projections of collective shadows such as 'seductress', 'bad mother', 'disobedient woman', 'adulterous wife', etc. However, in so far as these were collective shadows, she could not use them to be liberated from her Sisyphean hill of suffering. She could not possibly expiate these collective shadows because they were not her own, and because they did not alter her star status.

In despair, she attempted to use her own body to free herself from the 'collective mask of individuality' and, yet again, she failed. She told the world in her televised interview (for the BBC's 'Panorama') that not only did she have an eating disorder but also that she was engaged in self-harming behaviour. When I asked friends and colleagues what they thought of this particular revelation, I was surprised that they did not remember it. This is most startling because 'non accidental self injury', especially to legs, is a strong indicator of severe psychological disturbance and at least the professionals should have been struck by it. This means that nobody could afford to destroy their image of Princess Diana as a star, by remembering this disturbing symptom. All other aspects of her difficulties could be incorporated within a manageable picture of a flawed (and moving) star but this symptom could possibly have destroyed the 'collective mask of individuality' and bring her down to earth; but it failed.

Here is the relevant extract from the interview between Princess Diana and Martin Bashir which was televised by the BBC on 'Panorama' on Friday, 24 November 1995:

QUESTION: According to press reports, it was suggested that it was around this time things became so difficult that you actually tried to injure yourself.

DIANA: Mmm. When no one listens to you, or you feel no one's listening to you, all sorts of things start to happen. For instance you have so much pain inside yourself that you try and hurt yourself on the outside because you want help, but it's the wrong help you're asking for. People see it as crying wolf or attention-seeking, and they think because you're in the media all the time you've got enough attention. But I was actually crying out because I wanted to get better in order to go forward and continue my duty and my role as wife, mother, Princess of Wales. So yes, I did inflict upon myself. I didn't like myself, I was ashamed because I couldn't cope with the pressures.

QUESTION: What did you actually do?

DIANA: Well, I just hurt my arms and my legs; and I work in environments now where I see women doing similar things and I'm able to understand completely where they're coming from.

This point is not made in order to pathologise Princess Diana but to illustrate how resilient the image of a star can be. Even clear evidence of being flawed will either be incorporated within the star-image or simply dropped and forgotten.

FROM STAR TO ICON

Although the word 'star' has been used for a very long time to characterise celebrities, it is only recently that the word 'icon' has been introduced for the same purpose. Princess Diana was frequently referred to as a modern icon and it will, therefore, be useful to ponder on the meaning of her transition from star to icon. This is relevant because one of the most significant aspects of the public's reaction to her death and, more specifically to her funeral, has been the element of spirituality.

The word icon comes from the Greek verb *eikazo* which means 'to make like, to represent by an image or likeness, to portray' and hence *eikos* is 'like truth, i.e. likely, probable, reasonable' (Liddell and Scott, 1869, p. 429). The Greek equivalent of icon, *eikon*, refers to a pictorial representation, an image, a likeness. More specifically, in the Eastern Orthodox Christian tradition (to which the Greek, Russian, and other Eastern European Churches belong), an icon is a religious image mostly painted on a wooden board and used almost exclusively in devotional practices. Icons may also be produced through other artistic forms such as mosaics and embroidery.

Although it would be difficult to identify the precise reasons why the word icon has entered (with this specific meaning) the modern Anglo-Saxon vocabulary so recently, it may have to do with the fact that Western Europeans and Americans have been increasingly exposed to Russian culture and spirituality (culminating with the fall of communism). Many exhibitions of Russian icons have toured the major cities of Europe and the United States of America in the last dozen years and made a strong impression. In addition, Lawrence Durrell's book of poetry *The Ikons* (1966), and very recently the music of John Tavener (whose composition *Icon* was widely acclaimed), may have also contributed. The only dictionary that I have found which includes icon with this connotation is the 'Encyclopaedia Britannica, CD Multimedia, 98', where the two relevant entries read: 'an object of uncritical devotion:

idol' and 'emblem, symbol'. It is interesting that the word for a religious object has changed its meaning and became 'an idol', as an idol is the very opposite of the icon. For a believer, an icon is a representation of a religious reality, an authentic presence which is alive and felt as real, whereas an idol is a fake and empty parody. For a non-believer, of course, this distinction is not relevant and this is why in our post-modern world, with its characteristic stance of non-commitment, there is no difference between idols and icons.

Nevertheless, the shift to calling a celebrity an icon rather than a star would inevitably include an element of spirituality. Let us not forget that celebrities have also been called idols for a long time; this suggests that there may be a need to introduce some spiritual dimension to popular culture. The reaction to Princess Diana's death has demonstrated this need in a very eloquent way. However, what is specific about icons that can possibly shed some light on our understanding of this shift?

Icons represent a religious reality not in terms of providing a clear portrait or a crude translation of it, but in terms of offering an image and likeness of it. According to the art historian André Grabar, 'Byzantine images, . . . always kept their distance from reality. It is easier to understand the reason for this when saints or sacred events are represented [in icons]: the irrational is expressed by establishing a distance between the image and material reality' (1963, p. 32). But why such an irrationality and distance? This is because it is impossible to portray a sacred image in a simple, two-dimensional representation. As Mantzaridis, in discussing the meaning of the idea that 'God created man in His own image', clarifies: 'The "image" . . . is not confined to one facet nor is it fully represented by one aspect of human nature in particular, but is expressed and manifested, as though through a prism, through the whole of human existence' (1984, p. 16). This means that the image cannot possibly be a photographic depiction but would have to include an 'irrational' dimension which, therefore, would need to retain a certain distance from material reality. An icon attempts to convey a reality and at the same time tries to represent it. In other words, icons are not mere symbols, although they also have a symbolic function.

These unique characteristics of icons represent a more sophisticated and complex version of similar themes conveyed by the star image. Both stars and icons are distant, stable, unchangeable and do not have shadows (the images in icons do not cast shadows!); unlike other forms of artistic expression, icons are not subjected to the usual fluctuations, in terms of time, place, *Zeitgeist*, etc. However, as opposed to stars, icons are human creations and their unchangeability depends on a human effort to preserve the continuity of their reality. Both stars and icons refer to a reality that is not completely graspable by mortals. However, whereas stars are completely empty vessels, waiting to be filled by our projections, icons do have clearly discernible images which we can recognise even though they are distant and do not belong to the realm of our immediate material reality. Above all, icons are religious items created by people to be used in their religious devotion and hence the spiritual dimension is not an abstract one. Physical stars may also be associated with spirituality; however, their spirituality is attributed to them by us, whereas the spirituality of icons is immediate as they are integral to religious veneration.

Theologians of the Eastern Orthodox Christian tradition contend that one of the most characteristic aspects of icons is that they are based on the 'glorification' of God. The 'prism' that the iconic image is filtered through, is understood to be linked with the human need to 'glorify', a concept that requires some further elaboration. But before undertaking this, let us return to Princess Diana and note that it should be rather surprising that a person who was adored for her physical beauty, taunted about her sexuality and condemned for her adulterous behaviour would also be connected to spirituality. It seems that the image of the star could not accommodate this paradox. The collective mask of individuality emanating from the star image would have had a limited applicability and expression, whereas the image of an icon has the capacity to convey these complex antithetical qualities. Moreover, the concept of 'glorification' appears to be particular apt in relation to Princess Diana.

GLORIFICATION AND VIRTUAL SPIRITUALITY

Paul Evdokimov, in his classic study on icons, maintains that an icon 'radiates joy and sings the glory of God in its own way. True beauty does not need proof. The icon does not prove anything; it simply lets true beauty shine forth' (1972, p. 183). Icons cannot be rationalised away, outside the religious beliefs that produced them; they are integral to their theology and as such they are expressions of human gratitude to God. They are celebrating *the* true celebrity (not the host of mortal parodies) and they express the yearning to connect with the divine, not in an abstract or cerebral way, but in the context of a devotional reality; hence, in icons 'the combination of the artistic element and mystical contemplation produces a visionary theology' (ibid, p. 188). Thus, icons convey and express a quiet firmness and contentment which does not strive to impress or entice. This is perhaps what makes icons enchanting even to those who are not associated with Eastern Orthodox Christianity.

Their solidity and steadfastness radiate a mystery and a power which is most attractive in our post-modern and ephemeral world.

According to icon theologians, the meaning of the glorification which icons express lies in the restoring of the 'fallen image to its former state by uniting it to divine beauty' (Ouspensky, 1978, p. 180). The religious aesthetics which apply to icons address a combination of what is true, good and beautiful. Nobody can dispute that we all have a need to experience beauty, truth and goodness and to communicate among ourselves about them. This is precisely what the idea of glorification is based upon. Glorification is central not only to icons but also to other forms of religious expression as well as to other traditions (cf. von Balthasar, 1982–89). However, the icon seems to concentrate on the need for glorification in a particularly restrained but enduring way which exerts a powerful fascination.

There are millions of contemporary invitations in our society to celebrate the true, good and beautiful. A myriad of artistic forms and entertainment ventures, health and spiritual extravaganzas, vie for our attention and patronage. Yet it seems that the more we taste them the hungrier we become for the 'real thing'. It is in the dazzling dizziness of this landscape that an image with a universal appeal is desperately sought. There can be no 'universal' image as such, of course, outside the religious sphere, and our very insistence on such terms as 'universal' or 'global' betrays the yearning for real contact with this kind of image.

Princess Diana 'fitted the bill', according to the language of show biz. She was as 'universal' as one can get today, with exposure across most boundaries: geographical, cultural, linguistic, religious, ideological, racial, socioeconomic, gender and age. Being outside the sphere of usual ephemeral achievements, she was a star by birthright, so to speak; she did not have to earn stardom by excelling in any field of art, business or politics. Being of royal descent herself and marrying into the most known royal family in the world, she was a guaranteed 'natural' and 'stable' star. Thus, she had impeccable credentials. Her physical beauty and charm, in addition to her evident vulnerability made her most attractive. However, as her popularity grew and the world sniffed the possibility that a 'genuine' and 'universal' icon was possibly emerging, the hunger for the 'real' image seems to have got out of control and inevitably the spiritual dimension was added. Thus the star became the icon. In addition to her beauty, truth and goodness had to be grafted onto her. Her publicly displayed suffering came to her assistance and the pop idol was gradually transformed into a 'seasoned' icon. The collective mask of individuality must have created the right conditions for an identity that was constantly co-constructed and co-evolving between the personal and collective, to a degree that the private person and the public image fused into one entity, in complete harmony; one fed the other and nobody could distinguish them.

However, although the yearning for spirituality which the 'Diana phenomenon' exposed was genuine, the practice of it was more connected with the world of global media and instant culture. In a sense, what we witnessed was an outbreak of what could be called global 'virtual spirituality' rather than the committed spirituality which includes responsibility, personal connection, perseverance, endurance and wider applicability to life. Real spirituality provides the route for people to transmute pain and be delivered from suffering. Virtual spirituality, instead, amounts to participating in a spectacle which, although it may have euphoric and even healing effects, is of an ephemeral and idolatrous nature.

The term 'virtual' has interesting overtones because it is temptingly close to spiritual language. In this context it means 'approximate' and has been used in information technology to refer to Virtual Reality (VR), an experience through computers which gives the sense that one is physically present in three dimensional space. VR was first used to train astronauts and it now has wide applicability in technology and medicine as well as entertainment. Essentially, in VR there is nothing real; everything is 'virtually' real. As William Bricken, in an article on the Internet, puts it, VR is a reality that is 'as unreal as it gets'; nevertheless, 'VR allows mutually inconsistent environments to coexist without degradation. It both separates and includes. Overlay VR mixes the real with the virtual'. It is these qualities and paradoxes of VR that make it such a powerful paradigm for our times.

The funeral of Princess Diana was viewed by the largest television audience ever and attracted the widest participation on the internet. People felt that they were present at the funeral, experienced the real emotions of the bereaved and communicated through the internet their responses and feelings. The world participated in the drama and ceremony of her funeral in a direct way which, virtually, was experienced as 'virtual reality'. However, it was throughout her recent life that Princess Diana had attracted this virtual participation from people; her funeral just epitomised what had already begun earlier. Throughout, interlocked by the collective mask of individuality, Princess Diana and the world in 'virtual reality' they co-evolved a 'virtual spirituality'. Together, they formed the 'virtuous reality' of her life to a degree that at her funeral Lord Spencer felt the need to warn against the danger of allowing a virtual canonisation of her. Emphasising her human and frail qualities he attempted to restore the human nature of her individuality.

The unprecedented response at her funeral was overwhelming because it represented a unique combination of all these feelings and needs. The genuine expression of grief, glorification and spirituality, in addition to the host of other factors (from political to voyeuristic), made that single event acquire mythical dimensions. Her funeral seems to have confirmed her transformation from a star to an icon, allowing people to elevate her to a more permanent state of sanctity (or more precisely, 'virtual sanctity'). Now, unperturbed by the vicissitudes and oscillations of her personal life, as an icon, Princess Diana was offered for full veneration. Icons, as we have seen, restore the 'fallen image to its former state by uniting it to divine beauty'. Similarly, the 'virtual icon' of Princess Diana created a comparable 'virtual' effect: forgiving the folly of her personal life, people gave an astonishingly uninhibited expression to their need to glorify her icon.

FOREVER YOUNG, VIRTUALLY

Finally, there is a tragic twist even at the death of a star. If celebrity stars acquire the collective masks of individuality and do not own their own identity, personality or life, can they at least own their death? Ordinarily, at death, the narrative of a person's life comes to an end and his or her story gives shape to a life. However, with stars with the collective masks of individuality this, tragically, does not occur. Death does not bring an end to their physical life but marks a transition to another dimension within the media, as virtual reality. Death is not allowed to be the final chapter and conclusion of their life but it becomes a feature in their stardom. When Lawrence of Arabia was killed, people not only doubted the circumstances of his death but also doubted the very fact of it. There were rumours that the motorcycle accident did not actually kill him but was used as a ploy to allow him to change his identity and there were sightings of him in different parts of the world for many years. This is also the case with Elvis Presley who is considered by a group of his admirers to be living somewhere, happily incognito. Although it will not be surprising to hear soon of 'sightings' of Princess Diana, I thought that at least the public manner of her death would have precluded any conspiracy theories. Yet, such theories abound. Thus, if she did not own her life during her lifetime, if she was not its sole author, it may not be possible that she could own her death and speculation about who Princess Diana ultimately was is likely to linger on, forever.

Returning to the beginning, the 'forever young' and 'forever loved' themes can now also be understood in the context of immortality which inevitably the spiritual dimension of the Princess Diana phenomenon includes. Although it is absurd and even grotesque to consider immortality in the case of pop idols, once we move into the realm of icons and spirituality it becomes more plausible. Yet, insofar as the spirituality of the 'Diana phenomenon' is 'virtual', there is a puzzle: We know that stars eventually die and icons do not; how can a 'virtual' icon die?

REFERENCES

Bricken, W. 'Virtual Reality, As Unreal As It Gets'. http://www.hitl.washington.edu/publications/m-90-6/

Durrell, L. (1966). *The Ikons and other poems*. London: Faber.

Evdokimov, P. (1972). *The Art of the Icon: a Theology of Beauty*. Redondo Beach, California: Oakwood Publications, 1990.

Grabar, A. (1963). *Byzantium. Byzantine Art in the Middle Ages*. London: Methuen, 1966.

Jung, C. G. (1921). *Psychological Types*. *CW* 6. London: Routledge and Kegan Paul, 1971.

— (1928) . *The Relations between the Ego and the Unconscious*. *CW* 7: 123–227. London: Routledge and Kegan Paul, 1966.

— (1943) . *On the Psychology of the Unconscious*. *CW* 7: 3–119. London: Routledge and Kegan Paul, 1966.

Liddell, H. G. and Scott, R. (1869). *A Greek–English Lexicon*. Oxford: Clarendon Press.

Mantzaridis, G. I. (1984). *The Deification of Man. St. Gregory Palamas and the Orthodox Tradition*. Crestwood, New York: St Vladimir's Seminary Press.

Ouspensky, L. (1978). *Theology of the Icon*. Redondo Beach, California: Oakwood Publications.

Papadopoulos, R. K. (1990). 'Lawrence of Arabia: a Jungian investigation'. Lecture given to the *C. G. Jung Analytical Psychology Club*, London.

— (1997).'Individual identity and collective narratives of conflict'. *Harvest: Journal for Jungian Studies*, vol. 43, 2, 7–26.

Papadopoulos, R. K. and Hildebrand, J. (1997). 'Is home where the heart is? Narratives of oppositional discourses in refugee families'. In *Multiple Voices; Narrative in Systemic Family Psychotherapy*, edited by Renos K. Papadopoulos and John Byng-Hall. London: Duckworth.

Von Balthasar, H. U. (1982–89): *The Glory of God. A Theological Aesthetics*. (In seven volumes). Edinburgh: T & T Clark.

Wilson, J. (1989) *Lawrence of Arabia. The authorised biography of T. E. Lawrence*. London: Heinemann.

Tales of the Unfolding Feminine

ANN SHEARER

'It's almost as if she wasn't dead at all' said my local grocer bemusedly as we contemplated the racks of magazines whose covers still showed that glowingly beautiful face over and over again, weeks and months into the aftershock. In a sense, of course, he was right, for the 'Diana' whose image remained so eerily undimmed by Diana's tragic death had never been alive either, but existed rather as a conjuring of our multiple projections. Ever since we caught her in those first, shy glimpses, the princess-in-waiting, Diana had carried an archetypal charge. Now, in the unprecendented outpouring of emotion which followed her death, that ever-present archetypal world overflowed into our daily consciousness. Beyond and below all the diagnosis and speculation and tawdry revelation that has followed since, the events of that week still urge us to connect with something of that world of myth, which, says Jung, is 'the natural and indispensible intermediate stage between conscious and unconscious cognition' (Jung, 1995, p. 343).

We can sense something of the power of that intermediate reality in the wealth of individual reactions to the princess's life and death. Everyone has their own 'Diana'. For many people, the identification is just as intense as the antipathy seems for others; the very variety of their experiences tells us that it was indeed an archetypal image which seized them. What struck me, in the perceptions that analysands brought into our own analytic work, was just how often and how unerringly the collective reaction and the princess herself seemed to carry for them the image of their own healing. Not always, of course, and not unambiguously. There were echoes too of the public reactions to all the fuss that veered from indifference to bewilderment, to outright anger and even fear. Fairytale princesses and golden heroines have their dark and ugly sisters too. But overall, it was the release of healing energy through the tragedy of that death which seemed to carry the stronger charge.

So for one woman, who in the aftermath of her own tragedy had found neither time nor permission for grief, this was 'an excuse for people to show emotion' in a world that too often seemed to deny them the chance. For another, wrestling with her own hopelessness, it was hope itself that Diana had kept alive in her comfort of the suffering. For another again, the princess had carried the hardly-to-be-hoped-for truth that we can be loved for our vulnerabilities as well as for our strengths. A man who all his adult life has felt most bitterly cut off from collective values was seized by uncontrollable weeping as he watched the funeral, and he wept because he felt that at last he was part of something quintessentially English.

As for them, I suspect, so for countless others who sombrely witnessed the progress of that lonely catafalque or watched the televised event in a London that I cannot remember so quiet. In that intensity of silence, the rationalists' diagnosis of 'mass hysteria' could hardly, in any popular sense of the term at least, have been wider of the mark. Even after the funeral service, the mood lingered. Around where I stood at least, the huge crowds lining the Finchley Road neither pushed nor shoved nor stood on each others' toes to glimpse the coffin pass, but simply stood quiet and then, as simply and quietly dispersed. The whole event, which had brought so many out of their accustomed towns and streets and routines into a shared experience, also and paradoxically returned them to the privacy of their introspections; as one of my analysands said, it was a time 'when people could go into themselves'. Something extra-ordinary was happening – and it was something to which the collective ruling principle, the Queen herself, bowed in homage. To see the monarch *waiting*, together with her family, for Diana's coffin to pass, was to recognise that something altogether extraordinary was claiming attention. Just for those few hours, it really did seem that unity and meaning, both within individuals and between them, was not impossible. In the movement of the collective, to which the monarchy itself had to respond, just as much as in those individual glimpses of healing, it is perhaps not too much to speak of a projection of the Self.

'It is', said Jung, 'the function of Eros to unite what Logos has sundered' (Jung, 1927, par. 275). It is in this sense, it seems to me, that 'Diana' carried a truly *erotic* charge. Somehow through her image, as the individuals I've cited knew well, people were able to bring together parts of themselves and their emotions which in the logical world of everyday had become painfully separated. As for individuals, so for the collective. Over and over again we saw the princess insistently uniting what had been sundered, reminding the would-be efficient and competent world of public affairs of the weak, the struggling and the vulnerable. There was nothing *logical* about her approach, if logic has to do with the sensible discriminations of rationality; indeed, it was Diana's elevation of feeling values over reason that most alarmed her critics. But it was surely to exactly this *erotic* appeal that so many responded as if with a great hunger. This is a society where the erotic has become sexualised to the point where it sometimes seems impossible to understand relationship between adult and adult, adult and child, other than through that narrow and so finally distorting lens; we even call things 'sexy' when what we mean is that they attract, they energise. 'Diana's' attraction was not, it seems to me, primarily a sexual one; part of its power lay in a certain quality of androgyny. Rather, she mediated *eros* for us, bringing a psychic compensation to our over-logical and under-erotic lives and the force of its charge is a measure of how much we need it.

For Jung, *eros*, 'the great binder and loosener', 'the principle of psychic relatedness', was the foundation of the psychology of women, just as much as *logos*, that of 'objective interest', was fundamental to men (Jung, 1927, par. 255). Such formulations can make today's thoughtfully feeling and feelingly thoughtful men and women shudder indignantly, and I have done my share (Shearer, 1998). But for Jung, these two great forces, *logos* and *eros*, were also and more widely associated with, and expressions of, 'the masculine' and 'the feminine'. And it is the movement of 'the feminine' through collective reactions to 'Diana' that seems to have been the greatest attraction of all.

In the story of the past century of psyche's journey in the Western world, the struggle of feminine and masculine to refind their balance must surely be a major theme. The collective movement of the feminine has brought us from the first stirrings of the suffragist movement through the furies of the recent wave of feminism to today's hurts and bewilderments; it has shaped economic, social and political organisation; it colours our histories and psychologies and theologies too. There are a myriad facets through which this movement may be glimpsed, and I want to reach into the image-bank of myth and fairytale to touch on just a few of them.

There has been a fairytale aspect to the Diana story from the very start, of course – and often deliberately exploited too. For me though, this takes us not just to a never-never land created by the peddlers of wish-fulfillment, but to the archetypal world itself – the realm where myths are 'first and foremost psychic phenomena that reveal the state of the soul' (Jung, 1954a, par. 7) and fairytales 'the purest and simplest expression of collective unconscious psychic processes' (von Franz, 1975, p. 1). In the images that make up 'Diana', we can see reflections of that vast unconscious realm and learn particularly about the movement in our times of the energy we traditionally dub 'the feminine'.

When Diana died, that energy seized the very structures of power. Not least of the images conjured in the princess's funeral service, through John Tavener's *Hymn to Athene,* was perhaps also one of the least expected: that of the Greek goddess of war and peace. Athene hardly seems the most 'feminine' of goddesses; to many, indeed, she has appeared more like a god in drag. Her very beginning, born fully armed and shouting a war cry from her father Zeus's head, has been taken as an image of the overwheening power of the patriarchal order as it crushed the more ancient rule of the goddess. Contemporary Jungians have seen Athene in such muscular institutions as military heroics, Pentagon planning and American football (Stein, 1978) and look for her among women who run the Red Cross, become invaluable secretaries to male bosses and oppose the Equal Rights Amendment (Shinoda Bolen, 1985). She has been seen, like the Virgin Mary, as 'the statutory female on a patriarchal board essentially hostile to women and nature' (Begg, 1985, p. 131).

For me, such understandings do less than justice to this most complex of the Olympians. At the very least, the clear-sighted goddess, as energetic and far-seeing in war as in peace, urges us to look again at the way we delimit 'the feminine'. That said, the image of Athene – often stern, always wise to the demands of the situation, wielding her father's thunderbolts as skilfully as her distaff and shuttle – is not at all one that I would have associated with Diana, Princess of Wales. Yet as Athene's deeds and attributes attest, she is far from being a patriarchal stooge. Her especial wisdom is to scheme and battle always – and craftily! – to bring something new to the governance of the land. In helping Prometheus steal fire from Olympus, she brings about a redress of power from the gods to humankind. In her famous reconciliation of the old feminine powers with the new ruling order at the end of the *Oresteia* she makes possible a justice less vengeful. The *sophia* of this Goddess of Wisdom has to do with what in these days of ecological concern we'd call 'appropriate technology' (Shearer, 1998).

So Athene's purpose is to reform the art of government, to bring a new energy to the heart of the 'masculine' order of the citadel; she shows humans another way to go to war beyond random brutality and conflict. And for that, it seems, there is also a contemporary longing. In her life, the image of Diana as 'people's princess' carried messages between powerful and powerless, North and South. In her death it brought together in an extraordinary intensity not just monarchy and people, church and state, but highest ranking politicians, glittery pop stars, modest charity workers and more. When during the funeral all of them were caught up in the roar of applause that spread from the crowds to the Abbey, *eros* and *logos* seemed, however briefly, united.

Yet Tavener's *Hymn to Athene* carried also an image very nearly opposite to that of the powerful goddess, for the composer had drawn his text from Horatio's farewell to Hamlet, as well as from the Orthodox funeral service, and here it could serve Ophelia too. 'May flights of angels sing you to your rest', poor sweet lady, betrayed by a faithless prince, caught helplessly in the conflicts of the state, driven mad and destroyed by its corruptions. Athene and Ophelia: as Diana's coffin was carried from the Abbey, these, through the music, were the images that went with it. And here is a central paradox: the focus of unity that 'Diana' became grew the stronger for the very complexity of contradictions she contained. As we learned more of her real and fictitious selves and the legends around her grew, she carried for us an incontestable truth: that we humans must struggle with a mass of inconsistencies within ourselves and somehow learn to honour them.

Perhaps the greatest irony of his sister's life, said Earl Spencer at her funeral, was that ' a girl given the name of the ancient goddess of hunting was, in the end, the most hunted person of the modern age'. This is an age in which we are all more 'known' – to the scientists who can peer into our very cells, to the bureaucrats who chart our lives on their computers, to the psychologists who probe our depths – than ever before. At the same time, we are less known than ever in our pluralistic isolations, as more and more of us live alone and we lose the certainties of shared values and social assumptions. We yearn to be seen, to be understood, to reveal – and as what once was deemed properly private is compulsively poured into the public domain, the media even has a new shorthand for the phenomenon: the 'Dianafication of society'. Yet we long too to be 'given space', to be left alone, to guard something private of ourselves. In the hide-and-seek images of Diana – pursued, pursuing, evading, revealing – is a story of our times.

The great huntress Diana would have had none of that: she is the very energy of aloneness in her far mountain places, fleet of foot and as quick to camouflage as the beasts among whom she lives. When Acteon catches her at her bath – no long lens in those days, but a bush to crouch behind – she sets his own dogs on him to tear him limb from limb: the hounder hounded. Yet she also understands young girls in their fleeting, fleeing, longing-to-be-caught adolescence. In Greece, as Brauronian Artemis, she gives sanctuary to her young 'bearcubs', a place away from the city and its collective expectations, a space to grow up in before the demands of womanhood set in.

Most famous of her young charges, the one who most embodies the qualities of the goddess herself, is Atalanta, the swiftest runner in the mortal world. Her parents had hoped for a boy and exposed her on a mountain; Artemis sent a bear to suckle her. Unsurprisingly perhaps, the girl grows up wary of family life; she prefers the freedom of the hunt. But her father eventually reclaims her and her future too, insisting that she marry. What can she do? She agrees, but on one condition: she will accept only the suitor who can outrun her, all the others must die. So Atalanta, the swiftest mortal on two feet, fiercely protects her virgin integrity. But no mortal can hope to serve only one deity, and when Melanion invokes the aid of Aphrodite, the goddess gives him three golden apples to throw in Atalanta's path. How can a girl resist the enticements of love? She stoops to pick them up – of course! – and Melanion just pips her to the post. (Graves, 1955, 1 pp. 266–7).

Their story does not end happily. Is it Father Zeus who subsequently turns the urgent young pair into lions for making love in his temple, thus ensuring that they never make love again ? Or is it Mother Cybele who for the same offence yokes them to pull her chariot for ever? Either way, what Atalanta and Melanion painfully learn is that there is bound to be trouble with the parental Establishment when young people try to challenge it from within. Yet somewhere, too, Atalanta remains that untouched, fleet-foot girl, forever pursued, forever evading, forever just about to pick up the fateful apple: image of our yearning for both freedom and belonging.

Yet the apple must be gathered, Aphrodite cannot be gainsaid, Atalanta must put off her bear-skin and put up her hair. The young girl must go to the ball, the prince must claim his bride. Images of 'Diana' across the screen of years, from gauche young nursemaid in a droopy skirt to poised and glittering beauty: it *is* a fairy tale come true! The stuff of countless newspaper headlines, a thousand and more romances and numberless yearnings, these are the very images of our longing for transformation.

And so this is a story we can't stop telling ourselves, over and over again, in our different tongues and times. There are more than 500 versions of the Cinderella tale in Europe alone, it's reckoned, and countless others across the world, from Indonesia to the Americas; the earliest version seems to date from ninth century China (ah! that little foot!). Running through them all is an archetypal theme: the story of the young feminine dishonoured in her father's house, by the established order, exiled – often into servitude –

and finally redeemed in a sacred union of masculine and feminine, a new dispensation of love. Cinderella takes Atalanta's story on; she knows she must leave the parental precincts if she is to establish her own kingdom. But they are still sisters under the skin, these two, both still under the protection of Artemis. The earliest modern variant of the Cinderella theme is the Neopolitan *L'Orsa*, the She Bear, and the Lady of the Beasts still wraps the fairytale heroines in different pelts as they disguise themselves in their Catskin, Mouseskin, Donkeyskin, Pigskin, and even *Allerleirauh*, All-Kinds-Of-Fur (Warner, 1995; Philip, 1989; Grimm, 1975).

Over and over again these heroines set off, and their travels tell us of our own soul's journey from dark to light, unknowing to knowing. They carry the spark of transformative light in their very names. Our own Cinderella brings the Greek *ele* into sooty darkness; Finland has its *Clara*, Jutland its *Lucy*. Sardinia's *Barbarella* brings together light and *Barbelo*, which was a Gnostic name for Wisdom.

'Pursue Wisdom like a hunter, and lie in wait on her paths' the author of the apocryphal *Book of Sirach* urged his readers some 180 years before the birth of Christ. In our Cinderella tales we can still see traces of the fate of the great feminine principle of creation and hear echoes of our archetypal yearning for her redemption. As the Biblical Wisdom literature tells us, she was there at the beginning of the world, chief of works from the the start, delighting in the acts of creation. But the divine energic balance between masculine and feminine could not hold. The Christian Gnostics meditated on the fall of Sophia into the dark realm of matter and sought her redemption. Their tradition was carried by the alchemists who laboured for the transformation of gross matter into not literal, 'common' gold but a new synthesis of matter and spirit, a new world order. (And was not one of their best-known later texts Michael Maier's *Atalanta Fugiens*, in which the alchemist takes the legend of the fleet-foot girl as metaphor for the work?)

> Wisdom cries aloud in the street;
> in the markets she raises her voice;
> on the top of the walls she cries out;
> at the entrance of the city gates she speaks:
> 'How long . . .?'
>
> *Proverbs, 1:20–22*

At the end of a century of unprecedented upheaval in the position and aspirations of Western women, we are trying still to rehonour 'the feminine', both individually and collectively. Most recently and dramatically, we have witnessed the collapse, in the former Soviet Union, of materialism as both sustaining creed of governmnents and underlying explanation of human nature. In the current confusion of Western values, both personal and societal, can we discern again that yearning for the light – for the soul of the world which fell into the darkness of matter so long ago?

For much of that last, lonely journey to the Abbey Diana was accompanied only by men; in those measured steps we can see perhaps an honouring of the feminine at the heart of the masculine order. And 'Light's Beloved', and 'light's darling' the poet Carol Rumens called Diana in her lament for the princess's death. In the multiplicity of images of that radiant blonde that were 'Diana' in life shines our longing for transformation. In the myriad candles that illumined her death is our knowledge that transformation cannot come painlessly, that love's journey takes us into tragedy and darkness too, and that beyond and beneath the Cinderella stories is the oldest fairy-tale of all: the suffering of Psyche in her search for Eros, the archetypal story of the soul's yearning for love.

What a sight those candles lit! The mounds of flowers, the cards and messages, the iconic images of the princess, the processions of people: it was as if a wave of feeling from an older cult altogether had warmed our chilly, Northern soul. People saw visions of the princess, much as devout Catholics have glimpsed saints, or even the Virgin Mary herself; fifty apparitions of Diana were reported from around Kensington Palace alone. There was open talk of sanctity, even of formal canonisation. Those little candles, lights in the darkness, were fanned and fuelled as Elton John's 'Candle in the Wind' sold in its millions, until 'Diana' became an image of light itself. There was a collective longing, it seemed, to know that somewhere pure gold did exist, untarnished by the world. Both image and longing were burnished when, by one of those coincidences that may be more, they were thrown into stark relief by the darkest of shadows. Two weeks after Diana's funeral, a huge portrait of Myra Hindley in the Royal Academy's 'Sensation' exhibition was condemned with outrage and disgust, not just by the weeping mother of a child she had murdered but by Academicians as well. The painting was attacked, removed, restored, shown under guard. Another blonde, but this time as false as the first seemed true. Those countless loving images of Diana holding hands with children now found a brutal counterpoint: that notorious mugshot, that fixed, unchanging glare, was here made up of the prints of countless children's hands. In the depth of condemnation of that image, a measure of what was craved: a reassurance of the 'all-good' made the more secure by a perception of the 'all-evil'.

The soap-opera version of 'Diana's' story was now revisioned to appear the stuff of sermons. That short life's journey could be recast as an exercise in edification: the sufferings for a life of duty; the public renunciation of wealth and glamour in the spectacular auction of the frocks; the rededication of her sorrows to relieve the world's. It could read like the life of a saint – but one whose humanity reached out to touch people's own. By another of those coincidences which may be more, Mother Teresa of Calcutta, whose prayers had been offered in the headlines following Diana's death, herself died just before the princess's funeral. In life, the women had met; in the photographs, the height and glamour of the princess is intensified as she bends to speak to the tiny, indomitable old nun whose life had been so stoically dedicated to the care of the suffering poor. This coming together of such opposites, of the age-old tradition of self-sacrifice and the bright face of today's compassion, seemed to promise a new sort of sanctity, more easily aspired to by far. In those images, there was an evocation not just of what 'Diana' carried of 'the good' but of how accessible this thoroughly modern Mother made it for us.

How could that promise die with her? In life, the princess had mediated between so many opposites – 'the people' and the rulers, the wealthy and the dispossessed. Could she not now, begged those notes and flowers and candles, intercede for us to higher purpose yet, link us to that sense of whole-ness for which we humans seem programmed to long? Mediation and inter-cession has ever been a function of 'the feminine', the *erotic* activity of Jung's 'principle of relatedness'. The manifestations around Diana's death evoked its most numinous image in the Christian world. It is the Virgin Mary's especial function to intercede with her Son on behalf of her suppliants, as their prayers ascend in the smoke of their votive candles and the scent of their proferred flowers. When one broadcaster spoke so feelingly of Diana's funeral as her 'coronation' as Queen of Hearts, we were not far from the ancient images of the Coronation of the Virgin as Queen of Heaven itself.

This high honouring of the feminine throws a bridge across aeons, for 'Queen of Heaven' was also the title of the great goddesses Inanna, Ishtar and Isis all of 4,000 years ago. It throws a bridge between earth and heaven too, for in her uniquely glorified body Mary belongs to both. She is hailed as Jacob's ladder, on which Christ descended to earth and humankind may ascend to heaven; she is the neck which joins Christ, the head of the church, to the body of the faithful (Warner, 1976). In her Assumption, body and soul, she unites the realms and brings completion to the masculine Trinity. 'The three becomes four and the four becomes one', as the alchemists used to say. For Jung, the enshrining of the Assumption in dogma in 1950 marked a desperately-needed symbolic union between matter and spirit, prefigured in the alchemical imagery of the sacred marriage (Jung, 1954b, paras 195–7). In life, Diana carried the matter–spirit split in her own wounded body, and an image of its healing in her particular attentions to those whose bodies were ravaged by war or disease. In the response to her death, can we begin to glimpse a healing of that devasating split at the deep levels of the collective, a longed-for prefiguration of *eros* and *logos* in harmony at last?

'Great is Diana of the Ephesians!' was the ancient cry, for the fugitive goddess of mountain and forest was also the threefold Great Goddess, encompassing her own trinity of birth, life and death. *Di*ana: the Shining One – a people's goddess too, protectress especially of slaves. She is found not only in the wild and remote places, but at the crossroads along the journey. These may be points of major choice; they may also be simply the 'three-ways', the *trivia*, of everyday life. Has the death of Diana, Princess of Wales, brought us to an awareness of the crossroads, of points of choice, both large and small, personal and collective? The events of that week seemed to speak of a huge and unquenched thirst to love and be loved, a yearning for trans-formation and for contact with whatever lies beyond. These are among the most fundamental of our human longings. Yet the very intensity of the reaction to 'Diana's' death suggests that they have become dangerously neglected in the collective psychic economy. The choice of which way to turn is perhaps not trivial at all.

Television programmers must have given a good deal of thought to rescheduling the usual murder and mayhem for the day after Diana's funeral. What then could be more English and reassuring than Jane Austen's *Emma,* its young heroine's feistiness brought to order by good Mr Knightley, their marriage presaging – as he assures his faithful tenants – no change at all in the way things have always been done? To be sure, there was also *Strictly Ballroom,* a sparky cinematic tale of young love overthrowing tradition on the dancefloor. But that was in Australia, where they are known to like a change. We also had the episode of *Only Fools and Horses* in which the rascally Delboy embraces paternity to show that it's not just mothers who love. By the end of November, the Golden Wedding of the Queen and Prince Philip had celebrated for both rulers and people a traditional understanding of life's responsibilities, commitments and rewards. By then, too, Windsor Castle, seat of the monarchy and devastated by fire five years earlier, had been revealed in all the splendour of its restoration. It looked, said admiring commentators, as if nothing had ever happened to damage it. In the house of Windsor, all was as before.

With each month that passes, the deep conservatism of human nature strengthens its familar hold. It becomes easier to corrode the manifestations around Diana's death in cynicism than to cherish what did then seem somehow true. It becomes easier to accept the tarnish of gossip and revelation than to seek the symbolic gold that may underlie them. It becomes harder to hold to the psychic impact of those days as the tide of consciousness obscures the markings from a deeper, more timeless place. And yet, and yet, I find I do not want to forget the intensity of that week, nor to lose those glimpses of meaning from a world of myth and fairytale that knows more of us than we do ourselves.

REFERENCES

Begg, E. (1985). *The Cult of the Black Virgin*. London: Arkana.

Graves, R. (1955). *The Greek Myths*. 2 Vols. Harmondsworth: Penguin.

Grimm, J. and W. (1975). *The Complete Grimm's Fairy Tales*. London: Routledge & Kegan Paul.

Jung, C. G. (1927). 'Woman in Europe'. *CW* 10: 113–33. London: Routledge & Kegan Paul, 1970.

Jung, C. G. (1954a). 'Archetypes of the Collective Unconscious'. *CW* 9 i: 3–41. London: Routledge & Kegan Paul, 1959.

Jung, C. G. (1954b). 'Psychological Aspects of the Mother Archetype'. *CW* 9 i: 92–110. London: Routledge & Kegan Paul, 1959.

Jung, C. G. (1995). *Memories, Dreams, Reflections*. London: Fontana.

Philip, N. (1989). *The Cinderella Story*. London: Penguin.

Shearer, A. (1998). *Athene: Image and Energy*. London: Arkana.

Shinoda Bolen, J. (1985). *Goddesses in Everywoman*. New York: Harper Colophon.

Stein, M. (1978). 'Translator's Afterthoughts', in Kerenyi, K. *Athene: Virgin and Mother in Greek Religion*. Zurich: Spring Publications.

von Franz, M. L. (1975). *Interpretation of Fairy Tales*. Zurich: Spring Publications.

Warner, M. (1976). *Alone of All Her Sex: The Myth and Cult of the Virgin Mary*. New York: Knopf.

Warner, M. (1995). *From the Beast to the Blonde: On Fairytales and their Tellers*. London: Vintage.

The Death of the Heart

Archetypal Images of the Centre in a Time of Transition

JIM FITZGERALD

Of the images that appeared during the week of mourning preceding Princess Diana's funeral – that extraordinary week of suspended time, when a hair-crack appeared between conscious and unconscious in collective life, opened up by Death's chariot – several stand out for me. Chiefly memorable was the incongruous, stone figure of Queen Victoria. Outside Kensington Palace she is the young Queen, with sceptre aloft like an arrow pointing skyward, look-ing upright, confident and open, and very regal. To the base of this statue someone that week had stuck a simple, instamatic photograph of Diana, unadorned, with no trappings of formality or State.

The statue opposite Buckingham Palace shows a Queen in old age, bowed and sunken, the sceptre sagging horizontal in her right hand, a large, heavy orb – underlining her role as Imperatrix – in her left hand embodying the weight of the whole composition. Here she is flanked by angels and other symbolic figures, unlike the simple, unadorned statue in Kensington. Her face is serious, solemn and heavy with age. Overall, the effect is one of gravity and solemnity, that of the Empire and its burden. Under the lettering, VICTORIA REGINA IMPERATRIX, the simple poster had appeared, in one of its many mani-festations around the mourning places:

> LET THE MESSAGE THAT LIVED IN DIANA'S HEART
> FLOURISH IN YOURS FOREVER

As if to emphasize this message, the recurrent theme of the Heart appeared in many places. In one instance, a photograph of Diana, embellished with the Queen of Hearts symbol, appeared with the caption, 'The Queen of Our Hearts'. A frequent poster was the actual reproduction of the Queen of Hearts playing card, with such messages as 'The Best of the Pack', a pointed reference to the Royal Family. A makeshift poster especially caught my attention: 'IRELAND holds a special place in its heart for one with such a big heart'. The sentimental and the profound jostled for space in the vast proliferation of hearts and flowers, a kind of Valentine orgy.

In contrast to the stony queens on their thrones, the living trees became impromptu shrines to the heart, adorned with offerings of flowers, candles and fluffy toys. At the base of one, an impressive litany appeared:

> Queen of Care
> Queen of Peace
> Queen of Joy
> Queen of Courage
> Queen of Love
> Queen of Smiles
> Queen of Hearts,

and underneath all a huge red Valentine heart.

Queen, tree and heart, such powerful images, invoking archetypal energies at this time of crisis! A young man's message sums up the collective feeling:

> You were the heart and soul of the country.
> Your soul will live in our hearts forever.

The *queen* is the heart of the kingdom, however, and as the *axis mundi* she is also its central tree, the bole about which the kingdom revolves. What then is happening if Diana is regarded, and lauded, as the Heart and Tree, the 'soul of the country'? Who is this Woman who has replaced the central power of the kingdom? Young queen or old, she has supplanted both.

If the queen bee is removed from the hive, the hive sickens and dies. Similarly, the kingdom without a queen is sick and moribund. As many fairy tales testify, the absence of a queen is the issue that has to be resolved for the kingdom to flourish again. Psychologically, as Marie-Louise von Franz points out, the queen represents the principle of Eros in a collective, 'a style of relatedness to the unconscious, to the irrational, the feminine' (von Franz, 1970, p. 39). In medieval times, this role was played in the collective by the Virgin, the Queen of Heaven. The Litany of Loreto retains her royal titles, reminiscent of the Diana messages: Queen of Angels, Queen of Patriarchs, Queen of All Saints, Queen of Peace, among many other appellations. The recital of such litanies kept the collective psyche anchored in an Eros relationship to life and to its irrational well-springs in the unconscious.

Behind the image of the queen as consort of the king and that of the medieval Queen of Heaven, both of which belong to a collective modelled on the patriarchal structure of society, we dimly detect the more remote image of the Goddess. Throughout the Celtic world, and well represented in this country, goddess images are to be found, some independent of male consorts. Images of the huntress goddess Diana are among them:

Portrayals of Diana do occur in various parts of Roman Britain, and the evidence suggests that, in some cases at least, some native goddess is invoked in this classical guise (Ross, 1967, p. 277).

At times of personal and collective crisis, humans are led by an archetypal urge to re-connect to the images that well up from the collective unconscious as an expression of healing, of the continuance of life, even in disaster. These are archaic images, produced irrationally and spontaneously, to the bemusement of the rational mind. Decorating trees, setting up shrines and lighting candles, offering tokens and personal belongings, are all characteristic of an age long gone in England, but still to be found elsewhere in the world. It is as if nothing less than an ancient, long-forgotten folk ritual could answer to the psychological need experienced by many.

What was this need that surfaced with the news of Diana's death? Part of it seems to have been an aspect of a great collective shift which is being experienced all over the world, and is symbolized by the approach of the Millennium. In fairy tales, the aging king needs to be replaced by a young successor. By this, is symbolized the need for transformation in the collective psyche. For a time, the image of the Self finds expression in a way that keeps society vital and regenerating. But at certain points in time, there is a sclerosis in this image, and the necessity for renewal becomes imperative.

The messages and the images of Diana juxtaposed with the stone statues of Queen Victoria signify this unconscious movement towards a new Self-image. The whole modern era in this country has its origins in the stern repression of the Victorian era, ruled by duty and responsibility and the collective persona. The monarch is the head of the state, the head is monarch of the person. The head is the embodiment of reason, and life ruled by reason has evolved the marvels of science, technology, manufacturing, the reasonable fruits of materialism. What it has lost is a connection to the life of feeling, and its base in the non-rational psyche. In Jungian terms, the thinking function has reached its apogee in modern times. The solemn-faced Victoria is an apt symbol for this ruling function, adorned with sceptre and orb, the symbols of royal power, and of the rational, monarchical Ego.

'I shall remove the heart of stone from your bodies and give you a heart of flesh instead', says Yahweh to the Israelites, through the prophet Ezekiel (Ez. 36: 26). It is His promise of a complete renewal, in which the heart – that is, the essence, the Self-image – is transformed from a sclerotic state into an animated organ, through which the Spirit can again flow.

Queen Victoria, in her stony presence, well represented the whole Royal household as it was sensed by the people during that momentous week. The people asked for a sign, a token, to match the myriad tokens of their deeply-felt grief placed outside the Royal palaces. The empty flagpole on Buckingham Palace became a symbol of the hardheartedness of the monarch. Psychologically, the collective signalled that a central, axial shift was in motion, from Head to Heart as the vehicle for the informing Spirit. There was a collective need to have that reflected by the Head of State.

What is operating through the image of the queen at any particular time is the collective image of the Godhead. One could say, then, that up to the present time, that aging image was of a remote and stony Presence, demanding duty and responsibility, served by a cool, detached, conventional morality. With the advent of Diana into the Royal family, a corresponding shift, already prefigured in the collective, was hoped for within the monarchy; that is, the heart of stone might become a heart of flesh. In other words, the rational, thinking function might cede its place to that of feeling: a new image of the Godhead, merciful, loving, warm-hearted, sensuous even, might prevail.

The heart is defined in the dictionary, among many other things, as the seat of the emotions, of courage and spirit, and of love and affection. It is also defined as intent, will, purpose, desire, conscience, disposition, temperament and character. Finally, it means too, the innermost thoughts and feelings, one's inmost being, the soul, spirit. This range of meanings is an appropriate characterization of Eros or the feeling function. It also portrays the conscious processes and movements of libido in an ego grounded in this function.

'The heart has its reasons which reason does not know', said Pascal, and James Hillman formulates it slightly differently: 'The developed feeling function is the reason of the heart which the reason of the mind does not quite understand' (Hillman, 1971, p. 91). This paradox of mind and heart was aired in the letter pages of *The Guardian* during this time. The rational-minded were perplexed and repulsed at times by the obvious irrationality of the collective mourning process. What these people missed, and the rational mind always misses, is that the feeling function, although in crude and undeveloped form it can regress to cheap sentimentality, in its discriminated form is highly rational in its own right.

As Hillman states:

Although feeling does not operate in syllogisms, there is an exactitude and demonstrable reason in its operations. For example, one develops taste, which cannot be logically explained or experimentally proved but yet which is coherent and systematic. The ability to handle a problem or talk with a person in the right way shows a rational discrimination and an adjustment to what is needed. Yet the entire operation may not be intellectual (Hillman, op. cit.).

One is forcibly reminded of Diana, who confessed herself as 'thick' in the matter of intellect, but who developed an exquisite sensibility of feeling. One only has to remember the countless pictures of how she met people, of all classes and in all settings, and particularly the ill and the 'dispossessed'. It was this refined feeling function, to which she seemed to be born, which in her attained the condition of royalty. It was for this that she was called, over and over, Queen of Hearts. The function of feeling was revealed in her too, in that taste that Hillman mentions, of which she had an abundance. Often derided in this iconoclastic, cynical age, her self-expression through clothes was as immediate and authentic as was her feeling presence. This was a woman who was beginning to offer to the world an image of what a developed feeling function might look like, and thereby voiced for the age the deeper, archetypal shift moving obscurely, tentatively desired.

Already in the 1920s Yeats was attuned to the dawning realization of this desire for renewal in the unconscious:

> Consume my heart away; sick with desire
> And fastened to a dying animal
> It knows not what it is; and gather me
> Into the artifice of eternity (Yeats, 1965, p. 218).

Eliot, too, in *The Family Reunion*, portrays Harry as the sick modern man who needs a kind of spiritual rebirth from his conventional, stiff, upperclass family.

Harry discovers the curse that is on his blighted life stems from his family's denial of the reality of the heart. The redemption from this curse, revolutionary for its time, particularly for a member of his class, was to spend a lifetime in solitary exile, devoted to the service of the poor, the ill, the ignorant. (Eliot, 1961)

What these poets were intimating was a radical change of heart, a new expression of Spirit in life. Its expression can be sensed in the spiritual calling, in a religious attitude to life and in a dedication to others' needs. This was the path that Diana had seemed to be entering on in the months leading up to her death.

This death itself, in its manner of coming, in its unexpectedness, untimeliness, and violence, awoke another urgent need in people all over the world. Accidents disturb the secure order of the world. The advent of the unpredictable stirs up deep human fears of chaos. At this current period of transition, symbolized by the Millennium, the desire for a radical renewal co-inheres with a fear of ensuing chaos. This is the problem faced at all times of transition, in both the personal and the collective psyche: how to protect the transition from an old order to a new.

The fear of chaos is a perennial fear in humans, and humankind has developed rituals and festivals both to integrate the positive and to ward off the negative aspects of this chaos. On one level, this is the necessary fear experienced by consciousness when faced by the powers of the unconscious. Death represents the irrational, destructive power that threatens the ego and the conscious world. However, through the loss of religious ritual, humankind today is at a loss when faced with events that constellate the power of chaos:

We have forgotten the age-old traditions for dealing with chaos . . . Most adults living in contemporary society have never been exposed to patterns of dealing with chaos. They have never had the opportunity of observing how their parents or their grandparents dealt with chaos. Instead, the pretence of order and harmony dominates our images of the world. Chaos and its conscious experience are avoided. This is the root of our desperate clinging to order, and of modern humanity's helplessness and panic in the face of chaos (Wieland-Burston, 1989, pp. 24–5).

The appearance of the images of queen, heart and tree after Diana's death signified the search for, and affirmation of, a centering and ordering principle, a symbol with a mandala-like effect, as a protective device against the forces of chaos. Implicit in these images is the sense that the rational mind cannot bring the order that is needed in this situation. It is the heart and its affective sureties, that love is stronger than death, for instance, or that our moral values outlive us, or that the one who dies lives on in the hearts of others, it is these non-intellectual sentiments that create a sense of meaning and order out of what is experienced as meaningless. The heart here represents the voice of the ordering and protecting and sustaining Self as the heart of the psyche.

The icon of the pierced Heart, be it that of Jesus or Mary, represents the salvific value of human suffering and of the spiritual love, Agape. The heart is also a symbol of Charity, one of the Theological Virtues. As an image of secular love it is to be found everywhere today, a cheap and sentimental talisman. The heart and its vicissitudes is the recurrent theme of most popular songs, films, and TV soaps. The whole spectrum of Love, from sacred to profane, is contained in this one image of the heart.

Another need experienced with Diana's passing arose from the presentiment of a loss of connection to this human heart in public affairs. The urgent need for this connection had already been displayed a few months earlier with the public euphoria after the election of a new Labour government. Without a continuing connection to this heart, life becomes meaningless.

Diana, as a symbol of this human heart, performed an archetypal function for the collective. Since Reformation times, there has been a dearth of religious imagery, particularly of woman, through which both men and women might maintain a connection to the spiritual feminine. The Virgin's altar, her statues, pictures and feastdays have disappeared, leaving the collective with a divine King but no Queen. With the loss of this spiritual image from consciousness, as Jung says, the libido invested in it sinks deep into the unconscious to an archaic level. No doubt it was a logical outcome that the scientific revolution, with the concomitant numinosity of the material world itself, should have had its origins in this country soon after the Reformation. Matter took up the projection of the feminine spirit and became an object of investigation for the rational mind. This split – of mind from matter, of spirit from nature – has continued to the present. However, there are growing signs of the search, the hope, for a new form of relationship, a new *coniunctio*. The values of the heart, not those of the mind, have begun to be sought after and appreciated. A new relationship to the Earth and Nature is growing. We are witnessing a change of heart. I think it was this that Diana, as a woman of the times, equally a sufferer from the ills and neuroses of modern life, it was this new heart that she represented.

For men, the image of the feminine that Mary in previous times, and Diana recently, embodied and elevated for their contemplation, was that of the Anima. Diana corresponded well to the traditional image of the anima: fascinating, elusive, enigmatic, mischievous, fateful, animating. It is important for the man to keep the connection to his anima figure, and its loss, as Jung says, is experienced as a loss of soul. Meaning and vitality disappear from his life. The creative connection to the unconscious ceases, and he is left feeling the dryness and sterility of living. Many men were unexpectedly and deeply moved by Diana's death, as though they sensed the fragility of their own anima connection to the natural psyche. Their flowers and messages acted as a ritual of re-connection to this realm, a re-affirmation of anima.

For women, Diana seems to have represented what Jung calls the 'other', the 'inner friend of the soul':

This 'other being' is the other person in ourselves – that larger personality maturing within us . . . That is why we take comfort whenever we find the friend and companion depicted in a ritual . . . [I]t reveals our relationship to that inner friend of the soul into whom Nature herself would like to change us – that other person who we also are and yet can never attain to completely (Jung, 1950, par. 235).

Diana, as well as representing the Shadow for some women, also carried this 'other being' for them, that is, their Self-image. This created a real sense of intimacy with her, even at a distance.

It seems as if there was a unique conjunction in the person of Diana of the man's spiritual anima, with woman's Self-image. This would correspond exactly to the function that the image of Mary performed for the collective in medieval times. A harmony between these unconscious aspects of male and female was effected by the iconic images of Mary and Diana. In a positive way, this intimated a reconciliation, a *coniunctio* at an unconscious level, especially at a time nowadays when the relationship between the sexes at a conscious level is open to question.

I came across a book published after Diana's death, called *Dreaming of Diana* (Frances, 1998). In this, men and women from all walks of life tell of their dreams of Diana. The moving thing for me was the sense of the intimate place this woman had in the psyches of so many people. Whether as man's anima or woman's shadow or greater self, the wonder is that this one frail, fallible human being who was stumbling her way towards a collective role she seemed to sense dimly within her, was the single carrier of so many unconscious projections, and had a unique place in the psyches of so many people. What this burden does to a person can only be guessed at by most of us.

The bitter paradox is that human frailty cannot uphold the power of a Goddess, unless the flesh-and-blood woman is circumscribed and set apart by the full panoply of royalty and its rituals. By this she may be protected, as taboos protected the royal personages of old. It was the constant, profane accessibility to the public eye of the camera, the instrument of our own salacious curiosity, and the final stripping away of royal status (a symbol surely of the stripping of the victim before the sacrifice) that worked together to bring about Diana's downfall. It truly was a sacrifice, in which the guilt of all of us is implicated. It is the death of the heart, self-inflicted, for which, through books, and memorials, and investigations, we search for some final expiation.

We read the finished life now to discover some meaning in the short, blazing trajectory so characteristic of the *puella aeterna*, just as ancient astronomers searched the comet's path. Such a transient luminary has always predicted great social changes. Part now of the significant pattern that Diana offers to us, continuous with the life lived and the death encountered, is the actual place of burial. Diana's last resting place, as a permanent part of the natural landscape, will remain an icon for the future, the symbolic content of which may pass into the collective, to effect a gradual transformation. How we integrate the meaning of her life and the unique impact of her death is inevitably forecast in the details of her entombing. The *heróon* in ancient Greece was the tomb of the hero and later his sacred shrine and the reality of the psyche had its origins in the observances performed at such places (Bremmer, 1983). The collective psyche will transform and be conscious of itself in a new way by this inward turning brought about by Diana's death. Her desired place as ruler of people's hearts may be fulfilled in the mysterious way that death reigns in us through the afterlife of significant people.

To be in a continuing relationship to her who is now dead, the container for this memorial observance has to mirror the collective symbolism already released by her death. The choice of burial place could hardly have been more appropriate. She lies in the heart of England, on an island in an oval lake. The symbol of the centre is again evident. The island in a lake seems to have been a type of ancient ritual site, associated with the Goddess. One example is found at Silbury in Wiltshire. The island surrounded by the feminine body of water seems to have represented on the one hand, the baby in the mother's womb, and on the other, the body laid to rest in the womb of earth. Birth and Rebirth are identical, both effected through the body of the Great Mother, the Earth Goddess.

In Althorp, the lake is oval, and the egg-shape has at all times symbolized transformation, resurrection and rebirth. As a symbol of the Goddess from ancient times, the egg is in essence the heart of the Feminine, the creative womb. Collectively, humankind needs to shift from the old, phallocentric imagery of the patriarchy, back to this form of the feminine heart, the generative and nourishing womb. Delphi, derived from the word for womb, was the abode of the Goddess before patriarchy. It was regarded as the centre of the earth, and hence had its *omphalos* or navel-stone there. The womb is the speaking earth, the source of a wisdom of the heart and of nature that the solar masculine spirit, as expressed in the rational mind, fails to understand.

The death and burial of Diana happened in the middle of the sign of Virgo. She is traditionally represented as a young woman with an ear of corn, ripe for the harvest. This is none else but Persephone, about to be carried away into the depths by Hades, god of the underworld. Here she is to be initiated into the realm of darkness and will become its queen, before returning with the spring. It seems as if a perennial archetypal truth is here being expressed, the same that Jesus announced:

> In all truth I tell you,
> unless a wheat grain falls into the earth and dies,
> it remains only a single grain;
> but if it dies
> it yields a rich harvest (John, 12: 24).

The image of a Queen of Death seems alien to us, since we have lost touch with the psychic reality that the heart of generative life includes the seed of its opposite, death. This knowledge was at the heart of the Feminine mysteries, as our scant information on Eleusis suggests.

On the island where she is buried, Diana herself had planted a tree. It is one of a group of trees planted by people who were significant in her life – her birth family, her sons, her husband Prince Charles, the Queen and the Queen Mother. She herself has now become part of that vegetative cycle, in the shade of the royal trees. The tree is a primordial symbol for the feminine principle, and for the sheltering, nourishing and protecting aspect of the Great Mother. She is contained, not in some stone sarcophagus in a church building, but in Nature herself. Both Spencer and Windsor trees there may signify a reconciliation of opposites beyond the grave itself, not in the context of Church or State, or Royal accoutrements, but in the heart of nature.

In death Diana has already attained a new identity, different from that she had in life. Part of that identity is the legacy of feeling she has left us. A greater and perhaps more generative part is the continuing contemplation of her image, through which we touch the deepest levels of the unconscious. In this sense, she acts like the dead Eurydice, for whom Orpheus descended into Hades' realm. But, as Rilke points out, the identity of the one whom we knew in life will have already transformed into something more extensive, more cosmic and more fruitful, and how can we lay mortal hands on that?

Even now she was no longer that blonde woman
who'd sometimes echoed in the poet's poems,
no longer the broad couch's scent and island,
nor yonder man's possession any longer.

She was already loosened like long hair,
and given far and wide like fallen rain,
and dealt out like a manifold supply.

She was already root.

(Rilke, 1964, p. 41)

REFERENCES

Bible quotations taken from *The New Jerusalem Bible*. New York: Doubleday (1985).

Bremmer, J. (1983). *The Early Greek Concept of Soul*. Princeton: University Press.

Eliot, T. S. (1961). 'The Family Reunion', *Four Modern Verse Plays*. London: Penguin.

Frances, R. (comp.) (1998). *Dreaming of Diana*. London: Robson.

Hillman, J. (1971). 'The Feeling Function', in *Lectures on Jung's Typology*, von France, M. L and Hillman, J. Dallas: Spring.

Jung, C. G. (1945). 'Concerning Rebirth', *CW* 9 i: 113–47. London: Routledge & Kegan Paul, 1959.

Rilke (1964). *Selected Poems*. London: Penguin.

Ross, A. (1967). *Pagan Celtic Britain*. London: Constable.

von Franz, M.-L. (1970). *Interpretation of Fairytales*. Dallas: Spring.

Wieland-Burston, J. (1989). *Chaos and Order in the World of the Psyche*. London: Routledge & Kegan Paul.

Yeats, W. B. (1965). *The Collected Poems of W. B. Yeats*. London: Macmillan.

Making Men to Mourn

ELIZABETH GORDON

As I watched that lonely gun carriage carry Princess Diana's coffin through the silent streets of London, I was reminded suddenly of the death of the Amazon queen Penthesilea. Penthesilea, whose name means 'making men to mourn', came to Troy with fifteen of her handmaids to fight for King Priam against the Greeks and to avenge the death of Priam's son Hector. Killed in battle by the mighty Achilles, she was honoured and respected in her death as none of Achilles' other foes had been. When Hector died Achilles dragged his body in contempt around the city walls, but to Penthesilea he gave a funeral fit for a queen. Quintus of Smyrna, who tells this story, says that 'Achilles could not stop the pain in his heart' (Combellack, 1968, p.41). It seemed to me that the funeral of Diana carried with it some of the same feelings of Achillean remorse and pity that the death of Penthesilea evoked in the Greek heroes. Diana, too, had become in her death the fallen heroine, mourned by friend and foe alike.

The Amazons were warrior women. Sculptures on the Parthenon and around the Temple of Apollo at Bassae show them at war, fighting on horse-back and on foot, clad in short tunic and sandals, their hair hidden under crescent shaped helmets or small Phrygian caps. Amazon girls were trained from youth for battle, skilled in the arts of archery and horsemanship, famed particularly for the Parthian shots they fired in retreat across their horses' tails. The names of their queens reflected this equine, instinctual energy: Hippolyte of the stampeding horses, Antiope with face confronting, Melanippe the wild mare. Homer called the Amazons *antaneira*, women 'who fight like men in battle' (Rieu, 1950, p. 69). Aeschylus declared it no disgrace for a Greek to be killed by an Amazon on the field (Vellacott, 1956, p. 168).

When the Amazon women crossed the Hellespont and marched on Athens, it took Theseus and his army over four months to lift their siege of his city (Scott-Kilvert, 1960, pp. 33–4). Penthesilea herself was so fierce and dangerous on the battlefield that only Achilles, the greatest soldier of them all, could overcome her.

The women's movement of the twentieth century owes at least some of its inspiration to the Amazon archetype, particularly in the way in which the fighting spirit of the feminine has been constellated. Diana clearly demonstrated something of this spirit, most noticeably in the last eighteen months of her life. Here was a woman who vowed publicly in a BBC Panorama interview that she 'would not go quietly'. Among the many causes she championed, the one for which she will probably be most remembered was the struggle against the deployment of land mines. In intervening here she was, of course, also entering into a political minefield. She was challenging, as a woman and on feeling terms, the very masculine power complex of the international armaments industry. To see Diana, in her jeans, striding her defiance through the minefields of Angola was to see an image of the Amazon in battle. Penthesilea, too, in taking on the might and power of Greece, was nothing if not a 'loose cannon'.

The second thing we know about the Amazons is that they were outsiders, living, in the words of Diodorus Siculus, 'towards the ends of the earth' (Rothery, 1910, p. 110). The Greeks situated the Amazons in Libya, North Africa, in the foothills of the Caucasus but mainly in Asia Minor on the banks of the river Thermodon, where Heracles, Theseus and Jason with the Argonauts encountered them. In their distant settlements the Amazons lived an 'upside down life' where women held the power and fought in war. The settled, feminine world of Demeter's corn growing was not for them, nor was marriage ever part of their programme. Men, if tolerated at all, were kept in slavery – crippled at birth and set to household drudgery. 'We and the women of your nation would never be able to live together', a group of Amazon women told their Scythian admirers. 'Our ways are too much at variance. We are riders; our business is with the bow and the spear, and we know nothing of womens' work' (Selincourt, 1954, p. 308).

Diana so evidently felt herself to be an 'outsider'. Surely this was why she had such tremendous sympathy for the marginal and the marginalised – landmine amputees, homeless people, those who are ill with AIDS, all those whom her brother so movingly described as 'her constituency of the rejected'. Diana revealed her wounds to the nation when she spoke publicly about her eating problems and unhappiness. The same hint of woundedness lurks in the story, known to every school child, that the Amazon women used to sear off their own right breasts at puberty in order to fire their bows with greater strength. *A-mazos*, without breast, is one of the derivations of their name; *a-maza*, without corn, is another. In art, however, the Amazons are always shown as fully formed (Bothmer, 1957). Thus the issue is ambiguous. The wound acknowledged in the myth is hidden from the observing eye.

The Amazons, however, were not only outsiders and perhaps wounded. They were also powerful rulers of their own domain. Like their queens the royalty Diana expressed was of a different, 'upside down' and ultimately subversive kind. Her authority, she said, came not from the established order but from the feelings people had for her, from her position as 'queen of peoples' hearts'. On any rational and conventional level this was an absurd and bizarre claim, but as with the Amazon queens themselves, her influence was never lightly to be discounted.

The Amazons have always struck fear into the hearts of the establishment. One thinks of John Knox's famous tirade against the 'monstrous regiment of women' or, more recently, the American backlash against 'bitch power'. When, during the heady days of the French Revolution 'Amazon bands' of women took to the streets clad in short petticoats and little red Phrygian caps, even Robespierre decided that things had gone too far. 'All citizenesses' were ordered to give up their political activities and 'retire to their separate domiciles'. Their leaders, among them Olympe de Gonge, author of the famous 'Declaration of the Rights of Women', were sent to the guillotine (Gray, 1994, p. 71).

Did Diana stir up something of the same fear and unease? The imagery of the 'loose cannon', of the 'constituency of the rejected', suggests something unpredictable and unknown. We had, after all, never had a Queen of Hearts before. No one knew what she might do next. And no one knew the power of those whose causes she espoused, of the so-called disabled lobby, for example. We do not know how to cope with those whom we reject, the shadow elements at whom we dare not look too closely. Hence, perhaps, the pathos of that band of people, those in wheelchairs and those who care for them, who were allowed to follow in Diana's funeral procession but for whom there was no room in the Abbey.

Penthesilea by her example inspired the women of Troy to question their own passivity in war. In Quintus' poem young Trisiphone urges the other women to take up arms and fight alongside the queen. 'We ourselves too with brave spirits should take thought to share the battle. We are not much different from vigorous men. The sort of courage they have, we have too; our eyes and legs are the same and everything is alike' (Combellack, p. 35). It was shameful, she suggested, to leave the fighting to the Amazon alone. Diana's example, too, may have been inspiring and at the same time both uncomfortable and conscience provoking. At the very least it changed, perhaps for ever, the way that many of us now feel about so-called charity work.

The Amazon as fighting spirit was the disruptive and aggressive child of the war god Ares, the father of their race. But the Amazons also had a mother. Some say that she was Aphrodite herself, goddess of love and sexual desire – the original Queen of Hearts. Others say that the Amazons do not descend directly from Aphrodite but from her daughter by Ares, the nymph Harmonia (Graves, 1955, 2 p. 124). At all events it is from their mother's side, from their Aphrodite strain, that the Amazons inherited their youthful beauty and attraction for men. The connection with Diana is, perhaps, self-evident. She, too, seems clearly to have inherited at least a part of Aphrodite's girdle in which, we are told, 'all her magic resides, her Love and Desire and the sweet bewitching words that turn a wise man into a fool' (Rieu, p. 262).

For the hero of Greek mythology the Amazon may have been an enemy outsider, but she was also the object of his journey and of his desire. Those who encountered the Amazons on their journeys or fought with them in battle invariably fell victim also to their charm. Heracles, sent to the Thermodon to bring back the girdle of the Amazon queen Hippolyte, was greeted by the women with smiles, the golden belt offered as a 'love gift'. Theseus arriving in the same place fell in love with the queen – some say Hippolyte herself, others Antiope her sister – and brought her back to Athens as his consort. Most famous of all, Achilles, taking off the helmet of the fallen Penthesilea, beheld the beauty of the Amazon and fell instantly and tragically in love. 'Though she had fallen in the dust and blood, her face shone out under her lovely brows beautiful even in death. The Greeks who thronged around marvelled when they saw her, for she was like the blessed gods. She lay on the ground like strong Artemis asleep, Zeus's child, when her limbs grow weary as she hunts swift lions in the mountains' (Combellack, p. 41).

Quintus tells us that Achilles could not stop the pain in his heart. He also tells us that Aphrodite herself willed this because she wanted Peleus' son to learn to suffer pain. Not only Achilles, but also all his men, 'prayed that they might return home and sleep by wives like her' (Combellack, p. 41). When Thersites, whom Homer called the ugliest Greek at Troy, mocked Achilles for a weakling and a womaniser Achilles turned and felled him with a blow.

The time for mockery had past. The mood had changed. Penthesilea had fulfilled the destiny implicit in her name.

Pain is what we feel when we grow up, become conscious, when life changes, when we love and when we lose that which we love. Very often we do not realize our true feelings about a person until we suffer their loss. The process can change us irrevocably, can make us realise 'what it is all about'. Thus mourning can itself be a conscious-making process. It can change our attitude to life and at its best, can bring a new sense of value and meaning. In our collective mourning for Diana there seemed to be a sense of collective re-evaluation, a recognition that something important was happening to us, a feeling perhaps that we too needed to learn to suffer pain. In her image something of the Amazon archetype stirred us to consciousness, the harbinger of change and of a new value system.

But what of the Amazon herself? Is the woman caught up in Amazon energies destined always, like Penthesilea, for personal tragedy, for battles that she can never ultimately survive? Thus Hippolyte died at the hands of Heracles, Antiope fell defending Theseus against the invading Amazon armies. So strong is the connection between the image of the Amazon and the idea of early and tragic death that Mary Renault described in *The Bull From The Sea*, her novel about Theseus, the 'maiden rock' from which the women warriors would fling themselves once they had grown too old to fight in battle (Renault, 1962). Thus Diana's tragically early death can be seen as somehow inherent in the destiny of the woman possessed by the Amazon archetype.

There is, however, another end to the story which might enable us to see the Amazon aspect of the Diana myth somewhat differently. Not all the women died in battle. At a time when the gods themselves were young and Athene not yet born, the Amazon queens of Libya joined forces with the youthful Dionysus in his war against the Titans. The women marched with him in victory down through India but then demanded their share in the spoils of battle. Dionysus turned in fury, killing so many Amazons that the place was named *panhaemia*, the river of blood. Those who survived the carnage he chased to Ephesus, to the Temple of Artemis. Here the Amazons took refuge and lived on in safety.

Callimachus in his *Hymn To Artemis* tells the story thus: 'For thee, too, the Amazons whose mind is set on war, in Ephesus beside the sea established an oak tree and Hippo performed a holy rite for thee and they themselves, O Upis Queen, around the image danced a war-dance – first in shields and armour, and again in a circle arraying a spacious choir.' There were 'loud pipes' and 'shrill accompaniment'. The women 'with their feet beat loudly on the ground' and 'therein their quivers rattled'. So great was the noise of the dance that its echo reached 'unto Sardis and the Berecynthian range' (Mair, 1921, p. 81).

This is an image of transformation. It is as though the formation of the circle and the energy of this great dance around the image of the goddess became symbols of containment for the aggressive energy of the Amazon warrior women. It enabled them to turn their swords into ploughshares, to sacrifice their power in the service of the sacred. At Ephesus the Amazons never fought another war. They served instead as priestesses and votaries of the Temple. Statues commissioned to adorn the great Temple of Artemis, built in the fifth century BC, portrayed the Amazon at peace, resting on her javelin but still and settled in her new vocation.

Transformation is a word that has been used also about Diana. Since her death many people have commented on the way that she seemed able to triumph over her personal suffering and to turn that experience into service to others. It seemed that in the last months of her life she emerged not only as a 'woman in her own right' but also as a person with a sense of her own vocation and purpose. In her dedication to her chosen causes and to the land-mine campaign was it not possible for us to see those 'loose cannon' energies of the Amazon channelled into some kind of service to the sacred?

Artemis is the goddess who presides over child birth, engenders change and glories in the wilderness and outer reaches of this world. She has been called the Lady of the Wild Beasts, the Huntress, the Maiden of the Silver Bow and, in Sparta, the Lady of the Lake. At her father's knee the infant Artemis demanded gifts: eternal virginity, the company of women, sandals, short tunics and a quiverful of arrows. The femininity that she encourages is outside the normal domestic round, just as her groves are hidden in nature, away from the cities of men. They provide a healing space for her own followers where outsiders trespass at their peril, as Actaeon discovered when the goddess set his own hounds to destroy him after he had watched her bathing.

Callimachus' *Hymn* suggests that Ephesus was not only a sanctuary for the Amazon women but a resting place for the goddess herself. At Ephesus Artemis could rest from her roaming in the high mountains and the excitement of the hunt, anchored and grounded in a temple which was to become one of the wonders of the Ancient World. As the Roman goddess Diana, her cult was to flourish long into the Christian era. 'Great is Diana of the Ephesians' shouted the silversmiths of Ephesus in rebellion against the teachings of Saint Paul (Acts 19: 28).

Princess Diana's burial place quickly earned her the name of 'The Lady of the Lake'. In popular imagination that island in Northamptonshire has become a kind of sacred grove, set apart from the mainstream of life. In this process, perhaps we can also see a kind of resolution, feel its relevance. Perhaps we too need to find that healing space in which the energies of the archetypal Amazon can find rest and peace.

REFERENCES

Bothmer, D. von (1957). *Amazons in Greek Art*. Oxford: Oxford University Press.

Combellack, F. M. (1968), trans. Quintus of Smyrna, *The War at Troy*. Oklahoma: Oklahoma University Press.

Graves, R. (1955). *The Greek Myths*. 2 vols. Harmondsworth: Penguin.

Gray, F. du P. (1994). *Rage and Fire: A Life of Louise Colet*. London: Hamish Hamilton.

Mair, A. W. (1921), trans. *Callimachus and Lycophron*. London: William Hamilton.

Renault, M. (1962). *The Bull From the Sea*. London: Longmans Green.

Rieu, E. V. (1950), trans. Homer, *The Iliad*. Harmondsworth: Penguin.

Rothery, G. C. (1910). *The Amazons in Antiquity and Modern Times*. London: Francis Griffiths.

Scott-Kilvert, I. (1960), trans. Petrarch, *The Rise and Fall of Athens*. Harmondsworth: Penguin.

Selincourt, A. de (1954), trans. Herodotus, *The Histories*. Harmondsworth: Penguin.

Vellacott, P. (1956), trans. Aeschylus, *The Oresteian Trilogy*. Harmondsworth: Penguin.

The Living Symbol

Diana, The Media and The Archetypal Feminine

WARREN COLMAN

For many people, myself included, Princess Diana has become far more interesting since her death than ever she was during her life. Who was this person who could inspire such an enormous response in so many people? And was it Diana herself, the real living Diana as a person who was so special and extraordinary or was it the *image* of Diana created through endless media representations of her? The same question was asked about the enormous public mourning following her death: was it real or was it all a fantasy, an illusion, a form of mass hysteria? Were they grieving for Diana, the real Diana or for their own created fantasy of Diana?

As in Winnicott's famous paradox, Diana was both created and found. Newspapers and television are not a neutral medium between people and events on the one hand and the public who wish to know about them on the other. The media plays an active role in the creation of its own icons, shaping both the images it presents and the responses they generate. But they cannot manufacture responses that are not already there to be elicited, nor can they manufacture the icons on whom those responses are focused. Diana was not just a princess with a pretty face who was fashioned, Pygmalion like, into a media superstar in order to sell tabloid newspapers. Nor was she the ultra-special heroine she became for so many, just waiting to be found. The media needs the co-operation of its subjects in order to fashion its images. It is well known that Diana liked being photographed and was complicit in her media creation. She was, like many previous media icons, a spellbinder who became caught in her own spell. But unlike self-creations such as Noel Coward or Marilyn Monroe, she was not creating a part for herself which succeeded merely through the conviction of her own acting. She really was a princess but, at the same time, was playing the part of being a Princess. For reasons which I shall examine later, she was playing the part of being herself. She both created and was created by a media monster which then turned on her, devouring her in its ruthless hunger for more and more sensation. It is hard to say where reality ends and fiction begins. The divide becomes, as in Winnicott's paradox, a forbidden question: we must not ask 'did you find it or did you make it?' (Winnicott, 1951).

There is a quality of double-vision to this, wittily expressed in Bob Dylan's film, *Renaldo and Clara*. Dylan plays a version of himself called 'Renaldo' but most of the film consists of footage of actual Dylan concerts. In one of them, Dylan appears wearing a transparent mask and sings 'You could almost think that you're seeing double/When I paint my masterpiece'. Dylan's point is that while the image is inextricably interwoven with the real person, it is still an image. Even if the mask is transparent it is still a mask. The persona is not the same as the self even if, like the transparent mask, it has no features of its own. Dylan is and is not Renaldo. There is a further paradox here, a further double-image: Dylan himself is 'really' Robert Zimmerman and yet the self-created version of himself which is 'Bob Dylan' expresses his life and being far more than Robert Zimmerman ever could. Which one, then, is the real person? We think we're seeing Dylan (or we think we're seeing 'Renaldo') but the masterpiece of self-creation is the creation of a double-image which cannot be resolved back into its made/found components.

But whereas Dylan and other artists who have explored similar overlaps between real life and fiction (such as Philip Roth and Woody Allen) present art which is made out of life, with Diana it was effectively the other way around: as if real life could be made out of a media fantasy. Dylan, Roth and Allen are all saying: no matter how real this looks, it's not – it's fiction, it's art, it's entertainment. The media message about Diana was the opposite: no matter how fantastic and overblown this all seems, this is reality, this is life, this is really happening. Yet in both cases, the fantasy and the reality are inextricably interwoven. The media image is created in the transitional space of the forbidden question. The media is the public representation of the collective intermediate area.

Diana's death was a violent intrusion into this transitional space. As the sociologist Anthony Giddens put it, it was the intrusion of death into virtual reality. The link between reality and fantasy was broken since the real person who embodied the fantasy was suddenly, impossibly, no more. Like many people, my own reaction to Diana's death was shock and disbelief; not the disbelief of numbness and denial that often accompanies a sudden bereavement. I felt little or no sense of grief, personal or otherwise. I could not believe it because of an irrational unconscious conviction that *people like that do not die*, especially suddenly and in car crashes. *It felt unreal*, although ironically it was the brutal reality of the event which was so shocking.

Diana's death introduced an element of unexpected reality that brought such unconscious convictions to light and forced us to confront the forbidden question. Suddenly there was an outright clash between the fantasy of the special princess leading the charmed life of the immortals and the reality of a beautiful young woman killed in a car crash. Diana was made a saint but found to be dead. Out of this violent clash something new emerged: the transcendent function, massively amplified through the media of millions, bathed Diana in the radiance of the archetypes. A lived life, with all its unpredictable twists and turns became 'the story of Diana'. A myth is born.

In that extraordinary week between her death and her funeral, we were privileged a rare insight into the process by which reality is transformed into myth. We saw all around us, and were ourselves, inescapably part of a process in which the myth-making function of the psyche could be observed and experienced. In the face of the found reality of her unexpected, unbelievable death, we saw the enormous compensatory outpouring of the creative function of the psyche: the transformation of a human being into an archetypal symbol, a mere mortal transformed into an immortal goddess. Only then did it become fully apparent (at least to me) that this collective unconscious fantasy of the princess as goddess was the hidden engine which had driven all the media hoo-hah surrounding Diana throughout her adult life. Once the vulnerable mortal frame who acted as focus for this collective belief was destroyed, its unconscious elements were unleashed with unparalleled force: the wave of collective mourning, the overwhelming take-over of public consciousness constituted an outpouring of unconsciously driven fantasies for which the living human being no longer acted as container and limit.

On one level her death challenged the unconscious illusion of divinity through which Diana was perceived – for the immortals do not die. Hence my shock and disbelief. But on another, her death simply completed the process of deification. Quite literally, Diana was transported to another realm – not the real, living Diana but the Diana of our dreams and fantasies which, for most of us, was the only Diana we would ever know. Ironically, this was the Diana the real person had asked to be: the Queen of Hearts. Hubris, perhaps? Was her death the dénouement of a tragedy in which hubris is rewarded with downfall, in which the fates granted her wish only at the cost of her own death? But now I am making myth again. . . . At any rate, Elton John got it right: 'Now the stars spell out your name . . .'

* * * * *

One of the peculiarities of modern media icons is the degree of self disclosure and self-exposure that goes into their creation. Noel Coward and Marilyn Monroe constructed their images in order to *hide* their reality: the truth of Coward's homosexuality or Monroe's sexual abuse was to be eclipsed by the dazzle of their public images. But Diana's image was not tarnished by the revelations that the royal marriage was a sham, nor by her bulimia, nor even her adultery. On the contrary, these revelations served only to increase the media frenzy around her and added to her popularity. They did not enable her to escape from the public's archetypal view of her (as perhaps she hoped or expected); they simply transformed her from one archetypal image into another: if she was not Cinderella married to her Prince Charming, she must be Persephone abducted by cruel Hades or, worse, Judith tricked into marriage by Bluebeard.

Diana's capacity to embody archetypal fantasies for others was due to the fact that she embodied them in herself. She was a gift to the fictional world created by the media because she lived in that world of fantasy and tried to make it reality. Her own narcissistic need to perform, to be seen and to be praised created a desperate unholy alliance with the media machine's voracious hunger for more and more sensational revelations about her private life. She made the rest of the royal family look ordinary through her attempt to really be what the rest of the royal family knew they could only purport to be. She sought not merely to *represent* the archetypal glamour of royalty but to *be* it. She had to *be* the princess of our dreams because, para-doxically, she felt so lacking in herself. While for the rest of the royal family, being royal was ordinary reality, for her it was an extraordinary fantasy by which she was simultaneously enamoured and persecuted through her internal demand for perfection. She gave more and more of herself away, but the more she gave, the more the media demanded from her. In that sense the media *abused* Diana and those like her – they abused her need by using it for their own ends without regard to what that meant to her. *The Mirror* and *The Sun* do not reflect a beneficent loving image like the light in the mirror-ing mother's eye but a salacious, exploitative image which tantalises and eventually betrays those on whom their flashlights are turned.

It might seem then as if Diana was no more than the Queen of Narcissism, betrayed by those who claimed to adore her. During her life, this was much the view I had of her – seeing only her self-centredness, her destructiveness and her manipulation. Small wonder then that, in the wake of her death, I could not understand the sense of personal loss apparently felt so deeply by so many people. Perhaps there was more to her than I had realised? I began to read of her kindness, her compassion, her special feeling for ordinary people and to see that not everything she did was a performance for the cameras. Apparently, she was more than just a vain reflection of public adulation.

I realised that Diana was someone who had a remarkable chameleon-like ability to represent many things to many people and that this must have been part of her enormous appeal. She could have been merely a stereotypical princess but, by her refusal to conform to what was expected of her, she became an archetypal princess. Her iconoclasm and natural irreverence ensured that the images of her were sufficiently various and mutually contradictory to ensure that she could never become congealed into a stereotype. For anything that is fixed, solid, definite and one thing only can never be an archetypal image. Speaking of the archetypes Jung says:

The discriminating intellect naturally keeps on trying to establish their singleness of meaning and thus misses the essential point; for what we can above all establish as the one thing consistent with their nature is their *manifold meaning*, their almost limitless wealth of reference which makes any unilateral formulation impossible. (Jung, 1954, par. 80)

It is as if Diana broadcast on an archetypal frequency – her own immersion in fantasy and her need to be the object of collective adoration (the Queen of Hearts) enabling her to tune into the collective at a deep level. She reflected a multitude of desires, dreams and fantasies through which archetypal emotions could be contained and harnessed.

In the last few years of her life, Diana showed herself to be more than just a creature of her media image. Instead, she made and re-made the image into which she was cast, forcing the public to adapt their image of her as she twisted and turned within the royal trap, struggling to find herself and refusing to be pinned down to any 'singleness of meaning' (Jung, ibid.). Her determination to be herself offered real hope and inspiration to countless others. This was not just a fantasy princess, not just a persona image but a real person: behind the transparent mask it was possible to discern an individuating self. Only days before her death my own rather cynical view of her had begun to shift. She was reported in a French newspaper questioning why the media always looked at the negative side of everything she did. I began to recognise that I had been caught up in the denigration that is always the flip-side of idealisation.

The image presented after her death, (and uniformly agreed on by those who knew her), was that this was a new, more self-confident, happy princess. The work with AIDS, with lepers and with land-mines was conscious, deliberate and focused. This was a woman using her public position and power in the service of aims which were close to her heart, developing her own talents and beliefs and putting them to use in the context of her social situation. She was using her persona as it should be used – as a vehicle for expressing the self. Although she was still often the victim of the media, she had learned how to put her media image to use, not merely to meet her own narcissistic needs, but as a force for good in the world. In her later work, Diana was still using her narcissistic need to be seen but this was becoming transformed and put to use for more than narcissistic ends. This was a woman in the process of individuation

Diana did do a great deal of good work; she was kind and compassionate and caring and, in general, superb at fulfilling the role of constitutional royalty. But she should not be judged like Mother Teresa in terms of how much good work she actually did, since what she was primarily doing was communicating *about* goodness, creating a factitious image of goodness that is part way between factual reality and the living fictions of art and myth. Images of Diana exist within the intermediate area between subjective and objective phenomena. In the wake of her death there was a radical tilt towards the mythical as the image of Diana was cut loose from the wreckage of her death.

Many people have pointed to the idealisation of Diana, with the implication that it is *merely* idealisation and therefore not *real*. This reminds me of Jung's complaints about reductionism, the attitude of 'nothing but'. The 'Diana phenomenon' has taught me that there is always an archetypal component in idealisation – it cannot be reduced to 'nothing but' idealisation. We might say that idealisation is also 'archetypalisation'. That is, wherever there is idealisation, there is always an archetypal core. Fame lends to its possessors the glamour of being special, of being touched by stardust. But this glamour is archetypal – all those in the public eye are seen through numinous glasses. All of us use such people to receive our archetypal projections and, in many cases, they also actively evoke them, as did Diana, for their own narcissistic reasons. And when the mighty are fallen, when the great ones are revealed to have feet of clay and denigration sets in, this is equally driven by archetypal fantasy. If the great ones are not gods, then they are devils: there is simply a reversal towards the negative pole of the archetype.

This shadow side of idealisation was seen in the way the Queen and the rest of the royal family were reviled as the flip-side of the adoration of Diana. Ironically, Diana was idealised precisely because of her vulnerability and fallibility. Yet because the Queen did not display such qualities in public it was felt that she did not possess them. While Diana was idealised for making mistakes, the Queen was pilloried for it. Here, instead of imagination, there was merely fantasy. The Queen and the rest of the royal family were not allowed to be struggling, confused, ambivalent mortals like the rest of us – that would have been far too ordinary. In the world of archetypal perception, they must therefore be, if not the devils to Diana's beatification, at least scapegoats who could be blamed in some obscure way.

This was not the only aspect of the 'Diana phenomenon' that made me uneasy. During the week of public mourning, I felt confused and perplexed. I could not understand the scale of what was happening yet nor could I ignore it. In fact, I was *fascinated* by it. I was uneasy because I felt the stirring of collective unconscious forces, not only 'out there' but within myself and I was afraid lest I too be swept away by them. All this indicated that something powerfully archetypal was at work. As with 'idealisation', 'mass hysteria' is inadequate to meet the case. Again we must ask what the archetypal core might be.

Diana was essentially a *mediator*: she was not merely the creature of the media – it was as if she became its archetypal representation. Diana mediated between fact and fiction, between ordinary and extraordinary, between public and private, between the magical world of enchantment and fable and the factual world of everyday reality. She also became an intercessor for the weak, the deprived, the suffering and the outcast, acting as an intermediary between the powerful and the powerless. She was, of course, the anima: with her death, the nation was left grieving for its soul.

The anima is special amongst archetypes in that it is itself an image of what archetypes are like – that is, it is an image of the depths of the soul. Thus Diana's fluid, iconoclastic, irreverent attitude not only contributed to the archetypal potential of her image in general, but also gave that image the special character of the anima in particular. Jung speaks of the anima playing the role of leading the conscious self towards a deeper participation in life. Is not this what Diana wanted to do, tried to do and was seen to do for the staid establishment of the royal family, ensconced in a tradition that, while reassuring, was in danger of becoming atrophied? The anima stands always for life (Jung, 1954, pars. 56, 66). Here Diana also played the role of a trickster-anima: changing the rules, moving the goal-posts, up-ending the status quo in favour of change and renewal.

But more than this: in her representation of love and compassion, caring for the sick and needy, the outcasts and the pariahs, Diana played the typical anima role of embodying all that is suppressed and neglected in the outer attitude (the persona). She came to represent all that was opposite to the era in which she blossomed. Her reign was almost exactly coterminous with the years of Thatcher-dominated Conservative government, an era of ruthless self-interest, personal aggrandisement and the rule of commercial interests. Not only in her compassion but also in her beauty, she represented the value of everything that was contrary to the Gradgrind, utilitarian mentality of a world run by accountants. In her, people found an unconscious outlet for other aspects of their collective selves. She was the neglected, rejected, betrayed and forgotten soul of the nation uplifted to royal stardom. No matter whether she was *really* like this, no matter whether people recognised this consciously, or whether it changed their behaviour, the fascination with Diana went far beyond the usual ephemeral tittle-tattle of royal/society/ media-hyped gossip. Yes, there was all that in plenty, but the reaction to her death made clear that there was something more – something deeper that needed her death to emerge into the light of day.

In all the deification and the canonisation, it is essential to keep hold of the distinction between the person and the archetype she elicits. We know too much about Diana as a real person to be able to take seriously the claims of sainthood. And yet, before we scoff and scorn at the idea of Diana as saint, let us question whether the saints of the past were really so glorious and 'saintly' as they are now portrayed. Perhaps many of them were just as fallible, just as human, just as flawed – only their rough edges have all been smoothed away by the passage of time, their real lives refracted through a collective need for the numinous that transforms life into myth.

Some, but not all, of the people in the Park were unable to sustain this 'see-ing double' between fact and fable: for them the image *was* the reality. But we should not be misled by the concreteness of some of the claims about Diana any more than by the trashy sentimentality and prurient gossip of much of the media material about her. To reject Diana's significance because of this would be like rejecting Christianity because of the sentimental paintings and statues of Christ and the Madonna that are the stock-in-trade of many unsophisticated Catholics. The images of Christ and the Madonna may vary with the psychological development of the individual, but no matter how sophisticated or how primitive, the images refer to the same archetype.

The comparison is deliberate and, I believe, apposite. For some of those who were interviewed in the Park congregating around their makeshift shrines, the images of Diana touching the sick and the outcast had a virtually religious significance. They seemed no longer to be talking about a fallible human being but about the Madonna, the *mater dolorosa*, the font of love and compassion. More than this, there were hints of Diana not merely as the mother of God, but as the Goddess Herself, a female Christ: one who suffered with us and for us; one who touched the sick and healed them; one who was herself rejected, betrayed and, ultimately, crucified (by the media?). Some people may be shocked by this, or see it as a sign of the spiritual bankruptcy of our age that someone like Diana should be elevated to the status of a Christ. But I see it as confirmation of the strength and vitality of the archetypes and as a reassurance that archetypal needs will always find an outlet. The religious function of the psyche cannot be rationalised away.

Furthermore, I believe there is something exciting and radical about the idea that, in our time, it is a *woman* who is elevated to the godhead, bearing out the significance which Jung attributed to the Assumption of Mary in the Catholic Church. While the Church is still agonising about whether women can be priests, the collective unconscious has raced ahead and is already throwing up feminine images of the godhead. It has become possible to think of the Messiah and a woman in the same breath. And, more than this, it is almost inconceivable that a man *could* have done what Diana did, could express what she did and could have aroused the emotions that she did. Because what she *was* all about was emotion – especially the emotion of maternity and the feeling of love – the traditional province of the feminine. Diana as Goddess was radical in other ways too. The idealisation of Diana cannot be tarnished by any sordid revelations about her personal life or that she wasn't 'really' like that, since all those revelations have already happened. The idealisation *includes* these revelations; it is actually based on her imperfections. As one woman put it, 'It was her imperfections that her made so perfect'. There seems to me to be a radical transformation of public consciousness here that, despite the elements of archetypal splitting, indicates a shift towards a more 'depressive position' kind of thinking. Goodness is no longer split from error, weakness and sin. We no longer have to, or want to be spared the truth about our heroes and heroines. Rather, what we idealise is their human fallibility: not that Diana was saintly, but that she was not.

After two thousand years of sexless Madonnas, the historical legacy of a

Christianity that split sexuality from motherhood, Diana was celebrated as both a mother *and* a sexual woman. In the process, both images were transformed. Diana was beautiful and undoubtedly sexual but she was not sexually provocative. She went far beyond the anima qualities of her 'Candle in the Wind' predecessor, Marilyn Monroe. Although she was vulnerable to men and, in her Persephone incarnation, seen to be abused by them, she was no mere object of male sexual fantasy, luring and seducing men into sexual life. Judging by the crowds in the Park, she seems to have appealed to men and women equally.

If Diana was a goddess, ultimately she was the Goddess of Love. She combined in her person, and in her image, a range of mythical aspects but none can encompass her. It is this which makes her a living symbol. Jung defines a living symbol as 'the best possible expression for a fact as yet unknown or only relatively known' (Jung, 1921, par. 817).

The living symbol formulates an essential unconscious factor, and the more widespread this factor is, the more general is the effect of the symbol, for it touches a corresponding chord in every psyche (Jung, ibid., par. 820).

The public mourning offered a rare opportunity to cohere around a collective symbol, to acknowledge, albeit in disguised form, that we do have a soul and that it does matter; that there is a communal body and we do need to come together in it, if not to worship, then to meet the deep psychic needs which have traditionally been met by worship.

The amazing thing about the 'Diana phenomenon' is that it was there waiting to happen. A hidden community emerged out of the living room, away from the phosphorescent hypnotism of the TV screen and out onto the streets. It was a memorial in itself – a legacy of which the princess could be deeply proud, the tragically ironic fulfilment of the dream of the Queen of Hearts.

In the modern world there is a notable lack of religious ritual but in moments like this, we can see how people re-fashion tradition and create symbolic rituals for themselves. No-one 'decided' to create a sea of flowers in Kensington Palace or to shower the hearse with flowers as it passed; these things emerged spontaneously, out of a deep sense of need, a need to find symbolic tokens to express inner feelings. And it was the same with the books of remembrance that no-one will ever read. Yet people queued for days to write a few words in these books. From a rational point of view, this makes no sense at all – rational people tend to be scornful and dismissive, to look down on the ordinary folk who are led astray by their emotions, by mass hysteria. Not so Diana. She would have understood, she would have been there leading the throng. She was a woman who always led from her heart, not her head – often to her detriment. She was the patron saint of the feelings of those who publicly grieved for her in their thousands. Paradoxically, they grieved for her because she would have understood their need to grieve – she grieved for others in just the way they did. No matter if her own unconscious needs, her own unresolved conflicts and past hurts were all mixed up in the good she did. She led from her heart, not from her head. As an analyst much of my work is concerned with fostering responsiveness to the language of the emotions. It ill behoves me to be cynical about the mass display of public grief for Diana.

In my view, the dissenters who saw all this as mass hysteria and dismissed the crowds as people with sad, empty lives were missing the point. Of course dissent was suppressed. Of course the people asserted their deep longing to feel at one, if only for today. Tomorrow we will assert our differences, tomorrow we will return to the struggle to live together in a pluralistic society, tomorrow we will argue about race, power, politics and oppression. For today, just for today we will take the opportunity to feel what it might be like to be together, to feel at one, to share an experience with everyone else. This is a big one, this is an event we might not see again in our lifetimes. As I walked down the high street in St Albans on the Thursday and Friday before the funeral, I checked each shop for its obligatory notice 'As a mark of respect for Diana, Princess of Wales, this shop will be closed on Saturday 6 September until 12.00 pm'. And as more and more of these notices appeared I felt a sense of satisfaction. For once, the competition of the market-place, the religion of consumerism, had been trumped by the Queen of Hearts.

* * *

When I came to research this paper I watched several TV programmes about Diana. By far the most impressive was 'Modern Times', a two hour film shot entirely in the Park, observing and interviewing the crowds before, during and after the funeral. I was deeply moved by the sensitive, perceptive and wise comments made by many ordinary people who had come, for their various reasons, to join in the mourning. This was summed up for me by one quietly spoken, thoughtful man in his late 50s who was interviewed cradling a tiny baby on his shoulder. This is what he said:

I think that the people who have come to be part of it *are* part of it whereas before it always felt as though you were pure spectators to something else – it was what belonged to someone else. Royal occasions were royal occasions and we were just subjects to stand by. But this, I think, has been different insofar as people haven't just been spectators, they've been there taking part *in* it and I thought what was really good – that when Earl Spencer gave his talk it was the people in Hyde Park who stood up and applauded and the applause then went through the cathedral. It was the people who made the response and I thought that was good.

The transmission of these remarks to millions via the medium of television proves their point. A particular feature of 'Modern Times' is that there is no 'voice-over' commentary so not only is the spectator a participant but the observed is simultaneously the observer. There are no privileged observers, no special wisdom which exists outside the event. Nor is there anything I can say from my special position as a Jungian analyst that might not be just as well said by Joe Public in Hyde Park. Of course, we are *all* Joe Public and at the same time, we are all potentially wise commentators. We do not need the great and the good to interpret the event for us.

What was so unique about this occasion was that there was an enormous levelling of people but it was not, as so often, a levelling down but a levelling up. Ordinary people were, dare I say, sanctified by the occasion. The divide between those who know and those who are told, between those who speak and those who listen, between those who act and those who watch and applaud – Diana broke down this divide in life and obliterated it in death. She, the special one, the extraordinary one, the Princess – she is ordinary like us. Her death was the final proof of her vulnerability. She too, the immortal goddess, she is mortal like us. But what is more, *we are special and divine like her*. The sanctification of Diana would fail if it succeeded. Her real impact is to sanctify us all.

REFERENCES

Jung, C. G. (1921). 'Psychological Types', *CW* 6. London: Routledge & Kegan Paul, 1971.
Jung, C. G. (1954). 'Archetypes of the collective unconscious', *CW* 9i: 3–41. London: Routledge & Kegan Paul, 1959.
Winnicott, D. W. (1951). 'Transitional objects and transitional phenomena' in *Collected Papers: Through Paediatrics to Psycho-Analysis*, London: Tavistock, 1958.

Knowing Diana: The Media and the Need for Certainty

JULIET MILLER

'Directing in the cinema is literally being able to separate light from darkness and dry land from the waters. The director's power is such that it can create the illusion for him of being a kind of demiurge; hence the grave temptation of his profession, which can lead him very far in the wrong direction' (Tarkovsky, 1986, p. 177).

The extensive media coverage of Diana from her first appearance on the public scene as the shy bride of the Prince of Wales still continues after her death. This fascination with images and stories about the Princess has encouraged the idea that the media and, as a result the public, knew, in a private way, this very public person. The reactions of the public and the media not only reflect a powerful collective response to the death of a Princess but also reveal a modern fantasy that with more and more access to information technology we are able to know what is happening around us. This is a recent phenomenon which presumes that access to information automatically means knowledge and understanding.

Yet on 31 August 1997 the country was thrown into an unknown and confused state which we all grappled to understand and make sense of. The media were not able to maintain their preferred position as commentators as they found themselves drawn into the emotions erupting from the collective psyche. During the week between the death and the funeral, television, radio and newspapers seemed unable to think, or write, about anything else as they attempted to make meaning of something that they were unable to contain or understand. 'Are we united in grief or going collectively nuts?' wrote Joan Smith in *The Independent* (Smith, 1997, p. 23). It was as if they were faced with parts of the personal and collective psyche which they had never bargained for and never thought that they might have to take into account. A year later some journalists are still anxiously feeling the need to make sense of what happened. Decca Aitkenhead in *The Guardian* writes: 'now in a post-ideological culture, we have no model for making connections. All that is left is a muddle of emotion, easy to exploit and easy to manipulate' (Aitkenhead, 1998, p. 2).

After the death of King George V in 1936, Ronald Fairbairn wrote a paper about his patients' reactions (Fairbairn, 1936). He writes about how his patients' guilt and sadism is aroused and how the King's death stimulates their dread of losing or killing their own internalised objects. There is no suggestion however that the King is known in any other way by his subjects. His death is simply seen by Fairbairn as an important externalised event which produces extreme reactions in three of his patients and arouses expression of their unconscious parental objects.

In the mid 1930s the official media coverage of the King's death on radio and in the newspapers would have had clearly accepted boundaries and covered the sovereign's public role and the meaning of his death for the country and his people. Over sixty years later the place and power of the media has changed dramatically. Access to information of all kinds is considered everyone's right and the boundaries between private and public have become blurred or have disappeared. The Princess of Wales herself also helped to blur these boundaries thereby colluding with the media's insatiable hunger for information and images from either realm. Yet increased information, images and revelations did not mean that we knew or understood this woman whom we had never met.

The idea of not knowing and not understanding is a foreign country to the media; a territory that is presumed no longer to exist now we have access to all the information we want. Access to information presumes a kind of control and carries with it the idea that what we know about we can also possess. It also encourages the narcissistic fantasy that what we have access to and know about and think about, we have also created and own and therefore, as a result, as in the case of Diana, maybe also have the power to kill. Two days after the Princess's death Carol Midgley reported in The Guardian that Earl Spencer believed that every newspaper editor who had paid for intrusive pictures of the Princess had 'blood on their hands' (Midgley, 1997, p. 13).

Many journalists wrote of their guilty feelings: 'From the day she emerged blinking into the limelight when her engagement to Prince Charles was announced, we treated her like our private property' (Editorial, 1997, p. 22).

It is as if the tragic and untimely death of a young woman forced the media to look at their narcissistic belief that they create all that they see.

In *Memories, Dreams and Reflections* Jung describes his discovery that he might have access to thoughts that he has not created or consciously thought himself, through his conversations with Philemon, one of the figures from his fantasies: 'He (Philemon) said I treated thoughts as if I generated them myself, but in his view thoughts were like animals in the forest, or people in a room, or birds in the air, and added " if you should see people in a room, you would not think that you had made those people, or that you were responsible for them" it was he who taught me psychic objectivity, the reality of the psyche' (Jung, 1963, p. 207).

The response of the media to the appearance of the unknown and their confusion around this made me think about my own previous career in television and my reasons for becoming a therapist. I worked for many years as a documentary film maker and as my interests developed I felt more and more constrained by the medium I was working in. I felt it was one which required certainty and that this certainty underpinned its own powerful position and was as a result seen as essential. The idea of being in a state of not knowing was therefore very threatening. The creative state that Keats describes as 'negative capability', of being in a state of uncertainty without striving after facts, would not have been acceptable (Keats, 1948, p. 72).

Yet one of the fascinating things about film for me was the opportunity it gave for people to express themselves and for the viewer to respond to this in a dynamic way. I became interested in the imaginative space that could be opened up between the person filmed and the viewer. A space where something new might happen. Most of the films I made reflected individual and group struggles against frequently impossible odds and allowed people to speak and express themselves on film who would not normally get that chance. I never intended that the films should offer easy solutions or suggest that there might be only one answer. I hoped that they reflected the desires and determination of people who were battling to gain control over their own lives.

These films I made were never considered to be mainstream and it was always difficult to persuade editors to continue to support them. The films did not expound neatly contained arguments with an answer at the end, nor did they express an editorial opinion. I saw my role as attempting to reflect the feelings and situations of the people and cultures I was involved with. I could not tie them up neatly with a simple journalistic view because I wanted them to remain open. To allow an audience to experience without telling them what to think is one of the most liberating and exhilarating things that a documentary film maker can do.

I often had to persuade my editor to allow me not to cut an interview down to the bare factual statements because for me what the person didn't say or the length of her pauses communicated as much as what was actually said. But apparent ambiguity of meaning can be unnerving. We all like to know what is being communicated and place it within our own frame of reference. For the programme maker the temptation is to repackage the message received and as a result remain in control. But this is about knowing not from the guts but from the head and it preempts a sharing that is more than the communication of information.

Some of the television and films that I have most admired have resisted this attempt to organise chaos. They are rare and they carry with them a sense of danger inherent in presenting to the viewer a piece of work which does not have a single point of view. One such film, which had to struggle to be shown, was about the sacred city of Benares and how death is experienced in India (Singer, 1992). The film was long and rambling and had no obvious shape except the rhythm of a day from dawn until dusk. The film maker followed the activities of the people who lived and worked around one of the burning ghats on the Ganges. Bodies were burned, dogs scavenged, the manager of the ghat berated his servants, an old man descended hundreds of steps to take his morning wash in the sacred river. The sights sounds and incongruities of India were all here. For everyone who watched the film it probably communicated something different; delight, sadness, horror. But it was not prepackaged, it required the viewer to bring something to the experience. The producer of this film had to work hard to have it shown because the commissioning television company didn't understand it. Yet when this same producer was hospitalised shortly afterwards his doctor told him that although he had never thought of going to India now, having seen his patient's film, had decided that he had to. For the television company the lack of understanding was a reason to axe the film; for the doctor, who saw it, it became a powerful imaginative spur to experience India for himself.

Andrey Tarkovsky, the brilliant Russian who explores man's psyche and soul through his films, was uniquely interested in this process of wanting to be in the work rather than outside it. 'Personal bias must always be hidden: making a display of it may give a film topical relevance, but its meaning will be confined to that passing usefulness. If it is to last, art has to draw deep on its own essence; only in this way will it fulfill that unique potential for affecting people which is surely its determining virtue and which has nothing to do with propaganda, journalism, philosophy or any other branch of knowledge or social organisation' (Tarkovsky, 1986, p. 184).

Journalism does not purport to be art and needs to stand outside in its role as commentator or Greek Chorus. However the role of commentator is also held onto by the media as a safe place of detachment, of not getting into the alchemical soup and it takes an eruption in the collective unconscious to disturb this. The public response to Diana's death crossed a boundary that the media is fearful of. Suddenly it appeared that her death was not to be packaged and understood in the way previous royal deaths might have been. Her mercurial and tricksterish qualities of mixing public and private, conscious and unconscious were experienced as uncontained, emotional, exciting and sometimes frightening.

Maybe what was stirred by the death of the Princess was experienced by the media as outside their field of knowledge in the ways in which Tarkovsky and Jung describe. That understanding could come from an unknown source was seen as a threat by them rather than as an opening up of a new and creative space.

Some journalists did respond very concretely to the opportunity that it gave them to look at their profession . Two days after Diana's death the Press Complaints Commission began an urgent review of the paparazzi – an understandable response to shock – in an attempt to reframe the rules and contain the unknown. Maybe it also helped to assuage the guilt associated with a violent and shocking death.

Exploring uncertainty has never been seen as the job of the media. During my career in television it would have been difficult to find a television executive who would have agreed with Bion's suggestion that worthwhile knowledge comes through lack of structure rather than through carefully parcelled up facts: 'Instead of trying to bring a brilliant, intelligent knowledgeable light to bear on obscure problems, I suggest we bring to bear a diminution of the light – . . . The darkness would be so absolute that it would achieve a luminous, absolute vacuum. So that if an object existed, however faint, it would show up very clearly. Thus a faint light would become visible in maximum conditions of darkness' (Bion, 1990, pp. 20–1).

I am in my consulting room with a new patient who is expressing in a frenzy of anxiety and frustration that she doesn't know how to do this, how to be with me in the room, that all she knows how to do is to attempt to respond to supposed external expectations which she feels she always fails. She motions to her stomach and says she does not know how to listen to this and how frightened she is of doing so. She needs to know that this journey will be worthwhile otherwise, she says, how can she risk the uncertainty? She is asking for my reassurance and I have two simultaneous thoughts; that I do believe that it will be worth it and that I have no idea where we will go together. The difference between us at the moment is simply that I welcome the unknown and expect to bear the fear whilst my patient feels she has lost all her moorings. Thinking and knowing as a form of control has, so far, been her only way of relating to both internal and external worlds. I wonder for how long shall I be able to welcome the unknown before my desire for certainty defends against her chaos and I begin to impose an organisation on it. As Winnicott says: 'organised nonsense is already a defence' (Winnicott, 1974, p. 65).

Another patient with whom I am also beginning work presents me with the same question in a slightly different way. If I don't know where his journey is going to take him then how can he possibly trust me to help? If we are both in a fog at the moment then where on earth will the light come from to help us find our way? As yet he has not experienced the sense of what we may create together or the possibility of an imaginal world (Samuels, 1989).

This also makes me think of how my journey has taken me from one imaginal world to another one and how differently I experience them both. The worlds of film and of therapy are both interested in the emotional lives and personal histories of individuals. Both are interested in creativity and both are also open to an abuse of trust, the disempowering of the individual and a closing down on creativity. One reason I sought out a new world was my growing awareness of the distance between the people I filmed and myself. I can now see that I may have felt that in some fundamental way this could never be bridged, so the healing for me could not happen. However much I denied my role as film maker, that was what I was, the one who was expected to be in control and to know, to comment, to stand back and to model into shapes. As a therapist I am of course still tempted to do exactly this, but I know that if I can bear to be in the unknowingness of the work with my patient, then we may find a new way forward,

Princes Diana demanded a lot from the media. She wanted them both to stand back and comment and also to be in there with her and to bring the British public along too. Her mercurial qualities confused, excited and stirred up the collective unconscious and the media were not able from their position to understand and respond to this. They could not get in the bath with her. Nor could they stay outside it. Jung says this of Mercurius:' The elusive, deceptive, ever changing content that possesses the patient like a demon now flits about from patient to doctor and, as the third party in the alliance, continues its game, sometimes impish and teasing, sometimes really diabolical. The alchemists aptly personified it as the wily god of revelation, Hermes or Mercurius; and though they lament over the way he hoodwinks them, they still give him the highest names which bring him very near to deity' (Jung, 1954, par. 384). Diana has been both reviled and deified and the tension between these two opposites could not easily be held by her, the media or the British public. Who she actually was has not been revealed by her death, although our need for a deity to carry our projections has. 'What actually matters is how we saw her, not who she actually was' (Kraut, 1997, p. 1).

The media cannot exist without people and events. In a very fundamental way it feeds off the external world. It is its job not to be self reflective but to reflect society for the rest of us. However if famous figures become ideal carriers of our projections, it is our losses and our destructiveness that we experience when they die. Yet it seems we do not know this because we cannot face the pain of not understanding and knowing ourselves.

The life and death of the Princess of Wales continues to generate speculation in the media. On the anniversary of her death conspiracy theories abound in the press and television. The democratisation of information which the Internet stands for not only opens up the world to us all in a new and exciting way but also fuels speculation and misinformation at an increasing speed and gives them both apparent weight. As a result, the idea of the unknown becomes less real and less acceptable and the tragic and horrific death of a famous young woman in a Paris underpass will provide the media with material for as long as the unknown is unbearable and we continue to look for certainty outside ourselves.

REFERENCES

Aitkenhead, D. (16 July 1998). 'On how the heart rules the head in nineties Britain'. *The Guardian*: London.
Bion, W. R. (1990). *Brazilian Lectures*. London: Karnac.
Fairbairn, R. (1952). 'The effect of a king's death upon patients undergoing analysis' (1936). *Psychoanalytic Studies of the Personality*. London: Tavistock Publications.
Editorial (7 September 1997). 'Who does not have a share in this?' *Independent on Sunday*: London.
Jung, C. G. (1954). 'The psychology of the transference'. *CW 16*: 164–201. London: Routledge and Kegan Paul, 1993.
Jung, C. G. (1963). *Memories, Dreams, Reflections*. London: Random House.
Keats, J. (1948). *The Letters of John Keats*. London: Oxford University Press.

Kraut, J. N. (1997). 'The princess and the paparazzi'. *Jung Magazine*: Internet. http.//www. cgjung.com/articles/princess.html

Midgley, C. (2 September 1997). 'Editors in talks to curb paparazzi'. *The Times*: London.

Samuels, A. (1989). *The Plural Psyche*. London and New York: Routledge.

Singer, A. (1992). *Forest of Bliss*. London: Fine Cut, BBC2.

Smith, J. (7 September 1997). 'Are we united in grief, or going collectively nuts?' *Independent on Sunday*: London.

Tarkovsky, A. (1986). *Sculpting in Time*. London: The Bodley Head.

Winnicott, D. W. (1974). *Playing and Reality*. Harmondsworth: Pelican Books.

Your Cheating Heart

IAN ALISTER

A 36-year-old woman, tall and striking, walks into an old people's home and sits down at a table with a group of elderly residents. Seeing that they have been playing cards she picks up the pack and asks her neighbour with a giggle, 'Can you cheat?' Everyone laughs.

This woman is Diana, Princess of Wales, and this image was described to me by a female patient, also in her late thirties, as the piece of TV footage that imposed itself most powerfully in her mind out of the hours and hours that she watched in the week leading up to the funeral. She found it characteristic of Diana's original and creative qualities.

Diana's remark extended beyond the traditional comment of a Royal visitor and certainly represented her capacity to break down barriers and make us laugh, to make us feel close to her. Princess or commoner, we can all see the funny side of wanting to cheat. But even in using the words 'us' and 'we', I'm beginning to fall into an assumption that there is an universal response to Diana, or that in the collective response we are all feeling the same things. In fact, this story coming from my patient made me cross and after our session I began thinking that cheating can be a destructive defence born out of a fear of the consequences of facing reality.

Before exploring further this experience from my clinical work, I want to consider the idea that a collective piece of cheating may have taken place during the mourning of Diana: that her shadow aspect was all but denied in the public expression of grief and that some of us remain preoccupied because we still feel short-changed. In suggesting these two opposites – an intuitive creative Diana and a destructive cheating Diana – I want to try to reconcile them. If grief is swamped by sentimentality, its creative function, as an acknowledgement of feelings of guilt and a wish to make reparation, remains unfulfilled.

In the days after her death there were thousands of moving tributes to Diana's healing qualities, but there was little recognition of the woman who felt cheated of her mother, cheated of her husband, cheated of her role in a fairy tale and who ultimately was cheated of her life. (I notice as I write that I am inclined to use 'of' rather than 'by', as though it is Fate rather than human beings who may be doing the cheating). Most tragically, she has also made a significant contribution to depriving her own sons of their mother. An aspect of the tragedy is that the conscious priority which she gave to mothering her sons may have been undermined by her enactment of an unconscious malignant repetition. In some respects an awareness of the pains of her own childhood may have induced a powerful wish to act differently from her own mother; but if narcissistic wounds exist which are not acknowledged and worked through, the psyche may in part be damagingly pre-occupied with itself. When it becomes arrested in this way it can detach itself from the psychological and emotional needs of others and afflict them with its wounds.

Diana seems to have been unable to contain the intense conflicting emotions in her life, or to protect her vulnerable personal body from her own unconscious attacks which in part followed upon them. It is ironical that her death produced a ceremony in Westminster Abbey where unprecedented areas of difference were held together. The body politic, the body ecclesiastical and secular – clergy, politicians, media, celebrities, royalty, commoners, servants and children – were encompassed by the *vas*; the Abbey became the physical manifestation of the *vas*, or containing vessel, often referred to by Jung as essential for gathering in disparate elements which cannot be held by the individual mind alone. A homosexual rock singer played a pop song; a peer of the realm made attacks on the Royal Family and the Press and spoke of the effects of divorce, bulimia and low self-esteem. Earl Spencer received a standing ovation both in and outside the Abbey. There was an illusion in this ritual that the collective body of the nation could experience and survive the stresses that Diana as an individual could not. The collective unconscious demanded such consolation as a part of the mourning.

But the illusion was brief. Now the fragments are spinning off in all directions. However sincere the intentions of Earl Spencer, subsequent tabloid revelations have thrown doubt on his ability to carry them through. To hold the two sides of a wound together so that it may heal is a process that requires endurance of pain and conflict. There is an indication in both him and in Diana that the wish to repair is not accompanied by an adequate capacity to stand still and be self-reflective. The entire memorial process now shows signs of overreaching itself and attention is beginning to shift to the rehabilitation of Prince Charles and of the Queen in the eyes of the nation. At an intimate level the provisions of Princess Diana's will show a specific wish that her mother be involved in the upbringing of her two children. It seems a poignant cry from the grave, that perhaps her mother is still idealized, and that Diana never lost hope in her mother's maternal capacities but rather chose to provide her with a second chance.

In order to amplify some of these thoughts, I want to look at the way the Royal Family repeats a failure to marry things together, which becomes manifest in its difficulties in integrating what it perceives to be foreign elements.

In the abdication crisis of Edward VIII, over 60 years ago, there was a conflict between the steady, reliable – what I would call 'thinking' – qualities required by the collective institution of monarchy and the more unpredictable personal qualities – which I would characterize as 'feeling' qualities – represented by the individual. There is no shortage of 'conspiracy' theory about whether Edward was manœuvred from the throne, favourite of which is that the government was against 'foreign elements' being introduced into the royal structure. Whilst these 'foreign elements' took the outward form of the King's interest in German fascism and his devotion to an American divorcée, the inner 'foreign element' that was so feared was the King's perceived emotional instability and imperviousness to reason, as defined by the political expediencies of the day. To put it simply, Edward favoured feeling (Wallis Simpson) ahead of thought (his kingly duty). I suggest that Diana re-awoke this conflict in the House of Windsor.

Edward and Wallis Simpson were exiled to Paris where they lived until their deaths, after which their apartment was bought and maintained by a wealthy businessman with interests there: Mohamed Al-Fayed, father of Dodi. The Al-Fayed brothers are well known for the difficulties they have encountered in obtaining British passports. The possible religious and racial issues surrounding this seem to be connected to a fear of difference and of Islam in particular which stretches back through the Rushdie *fatwah* to the Crusades. The Al-Fayeds by contrast are Anglophiles, owning such quintessentially British institutions as *Punch* magazine and Harrods. I want to suggest that in Diana meeting her death with Dodi Al-Fayed in Paris, there is a synchronicity, a 'coming together' of the rejected, the exiled, the failed, which is a constituency to which the charisma of Diana connected.

In its more recent history, the Royal family has struggled and failed to integrate difference through the institution of marriage. Princess Margaret was dissuaded from marrying Group Captain Peter Townsend and later divorced the Earl of Snowdon. The three of the Queen's children who have married are divorced. Diana's parents were divorced, as is her brother. These facts perhaps only reflect the growing divorce rate. My emphasis is upon the manner in which society may increasingly be acting to split things apart, rather than focusing on processes that find different ways of keeping things together. I suggest that as a society we tend to foster a collusive inclination towards a destructive idealization which short-circuits creative disillusion. The former is most adequately represented by the tabloid press – Diana as a commodity – and the latter by social and political satire; it is interesting to remember that *Private Eye* was banned from the shelves of WH Smith in the week of the funeral.

An extraordinary feature of Diana's life, from her engagement to her death, was the extent of its public exposure, providing many personal details and characteristics which could act as pegs for our own individual projections. It had all the qualities of a soap opera except that this was real. We could watch this drama which involved the suffering and sacrifice of a person who carries a symbolic charge for most of us, whether consciously or not. We can feel it, think about it, and try to relate it to continuous psychological processes within us. To make sense of it in this way, to give it meaning, is part of our struggle to make body and mind whole.

Unconscious forces often appear in an external and dramatized form so that we may experience ourselves first in projection. By analogy, through linking this public, dramatic and externalized experience to what can be understood in the privacy of the consulting room, I will indicate an area in which I think psychological growth can take place through the emotions excited by the witnessing of suffering and death. In the absence of a personal connection, we discover an intimate collective one. The parallel to Christ sacrificed on the cross to save us all is not far away. The image of the cross is at the foundation of all my suggestions, in as much as it symbolizes the opposites that first have to be brought together and then kept together if a frozen and arrested state is to be avoided.

Some of my patients have mentioned Diana from time to time, identifying with her as a damaged individual, who struggled with the wounds caused by the loss of her mother, marrying a husband not fully committed to her, and again finding herself in a family where she did not feel properly included. There was also a fascination with Diana's body; how striking it was, particularly her eyes, how she controlled it, honed it in her fitness training, how gracefully she moved. How she enjoyed displaying herself – up to a point –

before the world's press, and how, behind closed doors, she attacked her body in bulimia, in self-cutting, in suicide attempts. It has crossed my mind that she was also drawn towards charities connected to violent attacks on the body – AIDS and landmines.

Whilst she sought and cultivated an untarnished reflection of her physical self and tried to eliminate internal blemishes through colonic irrigation and bulimia, she was also attracted to the maimed and the ravaged. Like other 'wounded healers', who unconsciously seek a plaster for their own wounds, she was more adept at applying plasters to the wounded other. Still trying to heal herself, she possessed an indefatigable determination to make others feel better.

I can see, from my clinical work with the patient I mentioned at the beginning, whom I shall call Caroline, how a fantasy of early narcissistic damage can be projected onto Diana; how deprivations such as an insufficient memory of a loving gaze from her mother and the fact that she didn't have a good experience of being handled, may have left her with an archetypal rage. How can we protect our bodies and our selves from the self-attack that is often the result of such a rage and understand that its origins may represent unconscious memory traces of experiences and feelings in the first months and years of life?

In her first session after Diana's death, Caroline told me that her immediate assumption was that Diana had taken an overdose. She was relieved, subsequently, to discover there had been a car accident, an act of Fate. Nothing further came of this observation until later in the week, just before the funeral. Then Caroline became keen to rationalize events, attributing blame and responsibility to every conceivable quarter save to Diana herself. The emergent idea that Diana might not be only a victim seemed too close for comfort.

Caroline's need to intellectualize and project responsibility was familiar. Loathe to recognize her psychic contents as her own, she would sometimes despair of an 'order' in analysis whereby her own internal processes would ever be understood by herself, or any other person. Neither of us was left in doubt that her level of agitation was unusually high, but we made little progress in our attempts to understand why.

Caroline's idea that Diana would probably end up killing herself stood out in my mind. It was not a thought I'd previously had. Now I found myself thinking about the dependent part of Caroline that was denied. When I suggested that she had also killed a part of herself she was resistant and I wondered whether I, too, had become a cheat by not interpreting her difficulties around issues of dependency, despite her mounting anger. However, her identification with Diana carried a new and immediate emotional reality for her which now existed between us in the room. Caroline could see how she, like Diana, drove herself into impossible situations, which in her case were often a repeated attempt to find 'mothering' in sexual relationships which were doomed to fail when she became too demanding.

As she watched the service in Westminster Abbey, Caroline found herself disturbed and shocked at the thought that there might not be a body in the coffin. A minute or two later she did have a sense of the body being in the coffin, but was unclear about which way up it was. She asked me if I knew, in an uncharacteristic state of heightened anxiety.

Caroline's idea was that the Queen had got rid of the body because she disliked Diana so much. Now we were able to link this to the attacks Caroline made on her own body, which were symbolic of a wish to assault a mother who she felt had not adequately admired and held her and who had failed to nurture her infant self-esteem. In our sessions she needed almost continual eye contact; I was a constant object whom she could reliably hold in view, but this could never be an adequate substitute for the crucial gleam in a mother's eye, which if consistently experienced and internalized, offers a quite distinct sense of ongoing well-being.

We were able to see a parallel with Diana's constant need to hold and manipulate the attention of the world's press. It was helpful for Caroline to discover, partly by using the couch, that it was possible to hold my attention effortlessly without having to keep me permanently in sight. This formed part of a natural collaboration which released a more relaxed and imaginative capacity in her.

Caroline's concern as to which way up the body lay seemed to be connected to a confusion as to whether she, or others, were responsible for the psychic contents that she experienced. She felt that if the body were placed upwards then parents and society were responsible and that blame or legislation were the remedies. If the body were face down, it would mean that a searching inside her own psyche was needed. Caroline's problems came out in her marriage where the demands of intimacy exacerbated her difficulties with separateness and with the relinquishing of omnipotent control of a partner.

In terms of change I question whether there is much potential from the top down. Clinical experience suggests that the capacity to become conscious of the power of archetypal and destructive drives involves a long and painful process. In my view analysis is more pre-disposed to change from the bottom up, recognizing the baby we each carry within, through a different experience of parenting.

It is not possible for this process to take place in a collective reaction. I believe that a central feature of the enormous public response to Diana's death was guilt, a sense that we all really knew in the back of our minds that a tragedy was developing and had enjoyed a voyeuristic interest in its progression. A later function of this response was to make an open and ritual reparation, in an attempt to elevate Diana to sainthood. In death the public gave fulfilment to the fantasy that Diana was deprived of in life. As one of the commentators remarked at the time, her funeral was her coronation. We each have our speculations as to the causes of the tidal wave of mourning: the sorrow at a life cut off, the triggering of a suppressed personal experience — perhaps even a relief that with her death the struggle was over and we would not have to choose between her and the Royal Family.

I'm struck by the way in which, in our mourning of Diana, we are returned to a reflection of elements of her first appearance. As an unknown kindergarten teacher she had suddenly emerged, raised up Pygmalion-like, and the country was swept along on an increasing and unstoppable tide of questionable, if heartfelt, emotion. At her death something of the same process was repeated, except that now she was hallowed. There was no stopping the tide, and little thought could be brought to bear. If you were anti-Diana last autumn you were well advised to keep your head below the parapet.

I took the title of this piece from Hank Williams' famous country song. Like many country songs it is about a complaining victim — it's always someone else's fault and never your own — the kind of thing we all like to listen to when we're in the mood. I'm interested in what a primitive and dangerous phenomenon the heart and all its qualities can be when divorced from its more sophisticated companion — the head. Without someone to watch over it from time to time — a function a mother performs for her baby and an analyst for his patient — it is vulnerable to becoming archetypally inflated, to cheat, to go its own way, to be worn on the sleeve or to cut down on safety measures — like the Titanic or the Mercedes — in a mad omnipotent rush.

Just as Diana was in a sense cheated by her heart last August, I wonder if we cheated ourselves of our capacity to think, to reflect, to hold different views, to be ambivalent, to be in the depressive position; to do all those things the auxiliary ego of a mother does for the baby. Everything was split; you were either for her or you were against her. If you didn't identify you tended to be regarded as a persecutor. Analysts all know how difficult it is to work in an atmosphere of splitting or abuse. It is hard to challenge a split state of mind – if you do not accept the innocence of the victim then you get saddled with the shadow of the attacker.

Diana possessed the most valuable feeling and intuitive qualities. I cried at her funeral because she was in part the queen of my heart. But she was also in Wonderland, the Queen of Hearts who, when crossed, screamed 'Off with their heads!', a royal prerogative but one which she could ill afford, when a good head on her shoulders was very much what she needed.

Along This Harsh and Lonely Road I Carry My Burden

MARY ADDENBROOKE

Several of my patients had dreams, in the time immediately preceding Diana's death, which retrospectively they experienced as having a pre-monitory significance. Maybe a lost thread, running deep in the collective consciousness, was ready to be tugged, and it is only one filament of this thread which I shall explore here. It centres around the need to tolerate the experiences of grief and lifelessness and the richness which can ensue. Archetypal themes were brought into the harsh and agonising spotlight as a result of Diana's death and hints, often overlooked, surfaced into people's consciousness, so that a new synthesis arose, albeit temporarily.

A patient had this haunting dream two weeks before the death. It has brought illumination of previously hazy aspects of her life to us and I am grateful to her for letting me write about its archetypal aspects. The dream had its own special and individual relationship to her life's pathway, as well as to her personal grief.

The dreamer is walking along a road carrying the limp body of a woman. The woman is not easy to carry, for her slim limbs flop about in an ungainly way so that the dreamer has to rearrange them. As she walks along the road she looks down again and sees that the woman is actually dead and she also notices that people, mostly men, seem to have come from nowhere and they are following her respect-fully. As she walks along towards her home, the crowd behind her grows. She fears that the road is endless, but finally she reaches her house and finds that it has a fine galleried hall. Figures, including her two sons, dressed in Elizabethan costume, are about to perform a play. There is a lively crowd all around her.

The carrier is walking along a road. No discernible features of this road stayed in the dreamer's memory. It is simply a road to somewhere and suggests the potential for progression or return. The feeling tone is of endlessness, as if the longed-for destination will never be reached. It seems to be neutral, neither helpful nor menacing to the central figures; much as a contemporary urban landscape may be experienced. This is of relevance, because this dreamer often gives vivid, colourful or dramatic pictures of the contexts of her dreams. Here, the backdrop is colourless and unimportant. This suggests that the road is a harsh and lonely place: it reminds me of walking either in a desert, or in an urban landscape where plenty may be going on, but in an impersonal way. The larger the conurbation, the more impersonal it can seem, until, if we are fortunate, we are able to recreate for ourselves something of a tribal community within the greater mass. The alienating characteristics of modern urban life formed the context of Diana's life too.

The chorus in Greek tragedies were commentators on the actions of the main characters in the context of harsh, implacable fate, personified as the gods. In the dream, the central dyad is not experienced as existing in isolation, but with silent acolytes who participate in the procession, just as the mourners for Diana played their part. The dreamer has since felt amazed that two weeks after her dream she found herself face to face with another representation of this image as she watched the figures of the princes with their father and uncle in the funeral procession, followed by the charity workers proceeding at a respectful distance. The dream depicts the classic theme of mourners in attendance.

Dream images seem all the more compelling if they are composed of more than one figure. Here, apart from the accompanying chorus, the central figures form a dyad. The part played by each figure complements the other. The predominant motif is dependence. One figure is alive, strong and active, the other is lifeless and dependent in the literal sense of the Latin word *dependere*, to hang from, to hang down. The limbs flop all over the place in an uncontrollable manner. Each member of this dyad needs the other to embody the phenomenon of carrying/being carried. One of the striking things about the dyad is that they are so different from one another, one lifeless, the other strong. This opposition mirrors dyads in mythology and folklore like David and Goliath, or the prince and the pauper. When we contemplate opposites in conjunction in this way, our mind can wander from one end of a spectrum to the other. The image invites reflection. In the dream no-one speaks. It is a silent procession. It is the grammar of the dream which is even more interesting than the figures. The central figures express a vital truth for humanity, namely that we need both to carry, and to be carried.

This juxtaposition of complementary figures was matched by certain paradoxical aspects of Diana's life. Perceived as vulnerable, she often starved herself in the most literal of ways. Of all her characteristics which were publicised in the weeks after her death, one of the most prominent was her involvement with people at the other end of the social scale; people who were also, but in different ways, victims. From a psychological perspective it may be that she needed the disadvantaged as much as they needed her, but this may also be true of many people who do nothing except feel uncomfortably guilty. Our motives are mostly mixed, whatever we choose to do. I was gripped when I saw a film of her talking to a homeless man at Waterloo, clearly a victim of too much alcohol over the years, and maybe under its influence at the time. Her straightforward tone evoked a straightforward response from him. Although there are, undoubtedly, other members of the Royal Family who have a similar gift of relationship, Diana was special because her persona so clearly declared the marks of an inner unhappiness. Rejected herself, she could bring happiness to others by involving herself with the socially marginalised. In the fragmentation of today's society, where image and status are so important, it is moving to see the contrast of princess and pauper. Divisions start to lose their clarity and loneliness may seem even worse in a palace. Vagrant drinkers and narcotics users often belong to a certain coterie and willingly share a bottle or a fix. It is both surprising and salutary to discover the hierarchy and fellowship amongst homeless people in any city; such hierarchies have a certain fluidity which I doubt exists in palace circles. Diana's empathy with the dispossessed liberated her from the straightjacket of protocol.

The dream motif depicts carrier and carried: two sides of one coin. There is less certainty than we might wish to hope for as to which side of the coin will be our lot in life. In the dream the woman carried is perceived as lifeless. I believe that Diana was able to bring a sense of liveliness to people who came in contact with her. This is what has made her loss so poignant. The challenge of how to achieve any independent autonomy must be enormous for any figure in the public eye, particularly for such an idealised and idolised individual as Diana. Global media communications accentuate a shadow side for superstars like her. She was the victim of prurient curiosity and in the psychoanalytic sense, projections which she could not live up to. It was, maybe, only a quirk of fate that her face and body had beauty, but it was no random chance that she was idolised by simple and sophisticated alike. Few of her actions escaped tabloid and media commentary: she was almost coerced into dependency upon her image – imprisoned by the curiosity and voyeurism of us all. Were we not saying to her, 'Everything's all right as long as you live up to our expectations'? Unlike the media, she was drawn towards helping powerless people, victims in a society which has little time for them. She reached out to the disadvantaged and forgotten; she touched the lepers and people who were HIV positive. Do we want to touch them? Intuitively, she knew about their needs to be touched and held. She reached the ones she wanted to reach. Most people had their own 'Diana' story which illustrated her generosity to the vulnerable; the television documentaries showed her glowing with light and humour in her interactions with people who were finding life intolerable. She cut through the formality that could have stifled her and those she met, by being direct, or even outrageous. She punctured the bubble of conformity by sizing people up, especially in their distress or embarrassment, and by choosing just the right approach. I enjoyed her question to a small child who was overcome with shyness and 'couldn't' present the bouquet or even approach the princess. Diana asked her, 'Have you got fleas?' Both collapsed in giggles. Something in the child was crying out to be noticed; Diana was able to do that. She possessed the gift of being able to make things better and make a link between herself and the other. People said, 'There was no-one quite like her'.

We all walk along a harsh and lonely road. The legends about Diana's care and empathy for the dispossessed gave us all a nudge to think about and even engage in dialogue with people who have become alienated, rather than averting our eyes. She gave us permission to care about 'shadow' people because she found common ground with them: trapped as she was. Sometimes when we are faced with the evidence of the misfortunes and suffering of others, we can feel at a loss and can retreat into a withdrawal that seems callous. In contrast, Diana embodied the archetype of the wounded healer. It is no coincidence that her interest lay in the rejected and I would say that this is a genuine function of the mothering process. Every mother needs to discover some way of coping with the less attractive aspects of her child, especially if she is tempted to reject those elements which are self reflective. I am struck that Diana was able to mother others, when she herself had had such an incomplete experience of mothering as a little girl. She asserted her independence most fiercely in this field. She refused to fall in line with royal families' custom of handing over children to other carers; there can have been few who did not respect her for it.

There are few contemporary figures who are able to build a bridge between the grossly diverse aspects of society with such grace as Diana. The carrier in the dream readjusts the load of the lifeless body so that she can manage to carry it better. As analysts one of our functions is helping people to discover better ways of carrying the unmanageable bits of themselves, whether that is by becoming better able to deal with the demands of a ruthless superego, or by recognising and using strengths which may have been denied or despised. So many of the ordeals and dilemmas we are called on to face in life initially feel quite impossible and remain so if we cannot discover new ways of being ourselves.

A classical Jungian way of addressing images in dreams is to see each one as a part of the self, and I hope to illustrate, with the help of the dream, a particular challenge which faces us. Redfearn writes about the diverse parts of the self, and the relationship of one to another within the self and the effects this has upon the individual (Redfearn, 1985). McDiarmid talks of feeling aware of different parts of himself interacting rather like a committee, an analogy which I have found to be of great help in the process of tolerating or even making use of the confusions and mood swings which can cause havoc at times within the psyche (McDiarmid, 1998). The picture of an inner committee, whatever its composition, is droll and intriguing and it facilitates a playfulness of ideas. One aspect of the self, however, which neither of these writers address specifically, is the aspect of lifelessness which is a part of our shadow.

As lifelessness is an important image in the dream, I shall focus on one or two of the many manifestations of this phenomenon in everyday life and of our attempts to deal with it. It is part of the individual shadow, and as such it is most often understood by its converse – a feeling of liveliness and well-being. Being able to tolerate feelings of lifelessness is a crucial life skill which remains one of the least understood, partly because any state of lifelessness, however temporary, has become anathema to our culture. Some of the anti-dotes, however, commonly used to side-step such a state can have damaging consequences, particularly those involved in its manic denial. People feel that they have to take action rather than wait for the feeling to pass.

The manic search for sensation is a dangerous proposition and one of the hazards which adolescents have to manoeuvre. If they are lucky, no lasting harm comes to them through their flirtation with altered states of consciousness, whether the high comes from driving too fast or from stimulants, or alcohol binges. Some are not so lucky. They come to serious harm through accidents of one sort or another while 'out of their heads', or their flirtation with alcohol or with drugs may turn into a full blown affair; a dependence which may not be so easily put aside. Diana herself had an all-too-short adolescence. It was truncated when her engagement was announced, and from being a teacher in a nursery school, she suddenly became the focus of national, and then international, interest. Later she seemed to have been able to empathise successfully with adolescents who had become marginalised in one way or another, although her own experience was untouched by material deprivation, and after her death there was wide reporting of the fact that, many homeless young people asked, 'Who will care about people like us now?'

The evidence of our current incompetence at dealing with lifelessness is all around us. A natural antidote is anger, but often at a price. Most psychiatric services today have access to assertiveness training or anger management groups which may help emotionally inarticulate people to get what they need from life without being destructive. For some individuals, however, it may turn out that they are generating negative energy in order to feel alive. In their case, learning how to be co-operative with others is a path to a greater sense of well-being.

The need for stimulation is innate. Those children who are valued by tolerant, accepting parents, who are sometimes willing to sacrifice their own narcissistic needs, will be more likely to grow up with sufficient capacity to accommodate their 'dead' moods and lifeless times. Then we may learn to trust that fallow times will follow and precede activity and awakening in a natural rhythm. But so much can go awry. Parents who are anxious and *too* intent on stimulating their children deprive them of such resilience and self sufficiency.

The voices of some current TV presenters of children's programmes illustrate how early the effects of the search for stimulation may start. There is a heightened pitch and very few pauses for breath, as if the presenters were terrified of losing the attention of their audience for one moment. Their continually animated facial expression has an uneasy quality because it is so unlike a conversation; animation without repose has an alienating and unreal effect. Some people found Diana irritating because she dropped her voice and her face and often made a little laugh before replying to any question. At other times she just said things with her eyes. Perhaps she was *willing* other people to speak — a rare quality today.

The lifeless parts of ourselves may be parts which we have outgrown. *Ennui* often ensues when one is living out something which needs to be discarded because it is no longer relevant. We often cling on after the sell-by date because the familiar is safer than venturing out into new ways of being.

There is something awesome about the sight of someone carrying a lifeless body. In the dream the crowd gathers respectfully, just as when the coffin was carried out of Westminster Abbey to the sound of John Tavener's *Alleluia, Song for Athene*. In states of grief, too, you feel lifeless, because you identify with the person who has died. Walking in a crowd, suddenly you think you have caught sight of them. I can think of few situations so alienating. There is a dream-like mist around you. No-one else can understand your search; everywhere you go you are looking, searching, scanning, almost unconsciously. You are lifeless and without desire because life has become devoid of all interest. The search drags you into a world of memories. All possibilities of change are banished because they only take you further away from the one you have lost. The tiredness, the sleeplessness, the lack of comfort or consolation have their own way of drawing you into another state of being. Kindness is noticed, but cannot cure. The search has to go on until it has run its course. Then in one mysterious way or another, often little understood, we come to feel less out of touch with the one we have lost. Once again they have their place within us. The relationship is resumed, even though the other comes to us only in thoughts, in dreams, in love. Reaching this point is a true purpose of mourning. But the time of grieving is a time when we need to rely on our own capacity to carry the lifelessness within. The bereaved may pass unrecognised. They may give few signs. They seem unreachable, cold and cut off, but there is so much going on within them. One of the harshest things said to me, after a time of mourning when I thought that I was functioning rather well, was that I had been unreachable. Of course I was unreachable. I was preoccupied with my own inner work and none of it showed, I suppose. It is hard work grieving; in its way not unlike madness. We have no chorus to warn us when our grieving time will come.

My patient's grief, as reflected in this particular dream, seems to have been principally for her mother, who died of tuberculosis when she was thirteen – on the brink of womanhood herself. She seems to have defended herself against the pain by amputating much of her memory of the happenings and emotions of the subsequent years. Now, to her astonishment, when she meets school friends she discovers how much they remember about that time, how many tiny details they have retained. Gradually, over the months in analysis, glimpses have come back with their feeling tone intact – most often it has been dreams which have brought the lost time to life. It seems that our capacity to withdraw temporarily at some level from what is happening around us when someone so vital to us dies is a benevolent, misty protection which ensures our survival. This is crucial to the mourning process. It is tragic to 'lose' portions of one's life history in this way, but perhaps part of what we lose in those states of melancholia would be unbearable and would otherwise destroy us.

Diana's death offered us collectively a chance to step outside the isolation of our remembered personal griefs. Our Western society has few rituals to protect us in the state of mourning. Those who know us are not unsympathetic, but they want us to be 'better' at a time when we may not be ready to do anything except grieve. It can feel as if we are letting our well-wishers down and this brings a painful sense of shame and failure. There is a terrible sense of exposure. But it was as if Diana's death released people from the cage of their inhibitions and gave them a much longed-for reason to mourn openly. What a liberating gift! To see the individuals slowly walking beside the flowers, looking thoughtfully at the children's drawings, the hand-written messages and the Valentine hearts. To be a part of that quiet procession, in London, walking to and fro on a sunny September evening, was an extraordinary experience.

Attendance at day centres for the mentally ill were reduced by *half* on the days immediately following Diana's death. There was an alternative focus for the pain and suffering and what is more, a 'legitimate' shared focus. Suddenly it was 'all right' to express sadness and loss with tears, and not to feel ashamed. Diana's death was widely grieved, and that, I believe, released many from the shame of sadness in a common acknowledgement of our inevitable shared vulnerability.

Even while all that was taking place, there were other darker tones to be heard. Much less uncomfortable to bear than sadness at loss is the other, angrier, face of grief: denigration of the dead, or of their significance, or the unremitting search for someone or something to blame. Who is responsible for this? Did Diana bring it on herself? These are all familiar concomitants of loss by death and serve to distance us from unmanageable emotions of sadness or vulnerability. It is much more comfortable to sit apart from grief by devaluing the life that has been lost. Regrets and recriminations spoke loudly after Diana died. This is another side of the story, but for many people it seems that however painful their grief, its expression was cathartic.

Grief and mourning find resolution once their purpose has been accomplished and it is possible to feel, once again, in touch with the one we have lost. It may not be a sudden neat resolution, but rather a sense of waking up and finding oneself able to experience the day in the old, familiar way, rather as one did before the death or loss. My patient's dream image expresses this more eloquently than words. The dreamer at last finds herself back at home with her two sons. In them, metaphorically, her future extends before her. Not only are they present, but there is activity and bustle all around. A play is about to be performed, a drama. Her life is indeed opening out. There is a gallery. This is an intriguing adjunct to a room, for apart from providing another level visually, it is also a place where music can be played or plays performed. If you stand above in the gallery, you can look down into the room and observe what is going on. Maybe you can eavesdrop, too. At the beginning of the dream, the dreamer is moving on a single plane – the road she walks along, seemingly endless. Grief can have a hopeless feeling of monotony. By the end she is dreaming of a scene where different perspectives can be envisaged and she can take up her stance in different intra-psychic spaces which may herald a return to full-blooded life. She has returned from her lonely walk along the path of grief, and perhaps because she has been strong enough to carry the lifeless figure on her own without obvious support from her followers, she can recover enriched. This is what happens if mourning is allowed to do its work. Times of profound emptiness may give way to a renewed awareness of life.

For me, there was something in the memory of Diana and in the response of the mourners which seemed to carry hope. In the days after her death, grief found an object for its clamour. In our materialistic society, alienated and lifeless parts of ourselves, which we hardly dare to experience, may be projected into the 'down and outs' whom Diana was not afraid to approach. I shall remember her as squaring up to parts of herself which some of us are afraid to face. The grief at her death was perhaps, in part, for lifeless parts of ourselves.

REFERENCES

McDiarmid, D. (1998). *A personal communication*.
Redfearn, J. W. T. (1985). *My Self, My Many Selves*. London: Library of Analytical Psychology, Academic Press..
Redfearn, J. W. T. (1992). *The Exploding Self: The Creative and Destructive Nucleus of the Personality*. Wilmette, Illinois: Chiron Publications.

On Not Living Happily Ever After

PETER TATHAM

'. . . and so they lived happily ever after', reads the parent at bedtime, finishing the story and closing the book of fairy tales. But can people live happily ever after? Have they ever, and do they now? Or are present day children tricked into believing this anodyne ending, which is often untrue to the nature of fairy tales and of life?

Look through the Grimm brothers collection (1975) and you will certainly find a number that suggest it. 'Then all anxiety was at an end, and they lived together in perfect happiness (*Hansel and Gretel*); '. . . and they lived for a long time afterwards, happy and contented' (*Rapunzel*). But, because human life is finite, happiness will never be for ever, and so others say 'and after the King's death, Dummling inherited his kingdom and lived for a long time, contentedly with his wife' (*The Golden Goose*); 'So he received the crown and has ruled wisely for a length of time' (*The Three Feathers*); 'thereupon the marriage was solemnised, and they lived happily until their death' (*Allerleirauh*); 'and they embraced and kissed each other, and went joyfully home' (*The Seven Ravens*). For some of the characters, however, the end is tragic. 'Immediately the physician fell on the ground, and now he himself was in the hands of Death' (*Godfather Death*); 'as a punishment, the wicked mother-in law was bound to the stake and burnt to ashes' (*The Six Swans*); Snow White's stepmother 'was forced to put on the red-hot shoes and dance until she dropped down dead'. Old time storytellers knew, it seems, that life is never one-dimensional, accustomed as they were to ever recurring tragedy, to seven lean years following on the full ones, to good fortunes dashed, and lightning striking twice at least. That was the way of their rough and unpredictable world.

To live happily ever after was not given either to Diana Princess of Wales. Here was a fairy tale princess, a Cinderella, whose life had been happy – but only for a while. In this she was indeed a heroine for our times.

C. G. Jung said of fairy tales that the characters and their adventures provided an expression of universal archetypes, or archaic images that have existed within human minds since remote times (Jung, 1954a, pars. 5–7). Such tales therefore might be seen as presenting, from the storehouse of the unconscious mind, universal themes and motifs compensatory to the conscious individual as well as collective attitudes and problems of the audiences to whom such stories were told. A consciousness that has become one-sidedly fixated may be livened again by the advent of such themes. Such a motif might itself be recognisable in any tale of an old and worn out king whose kingdom needed restoration by the appearance of a young hero who slays demons and rescues treasure. 'Hero', in this context, does not necessarily imply a male figure. Diana became just such a fresh source of vitality injected into a staid Royal setting that often seemed resistant to change. She did so by open refusal to abide by traditional 'rules', and a willingness to lend her name and presence to unfashionable or unacceptable causes, as well as the ways in which she did so.

The people of those earlier times were immersed in a world of imagination: this was an age of spirits and presences, none the less 'real' for all that. Though today's world is supposedly a more secular one, maybe our times are not so different after all, for many people still come home from work, longing for present day versions of the folk tales with their happy and unhappy endings. Our story tellers operate from within the radio or television set, as we watch the latest instalment of a favourite soap opera, whose several overlapping stories urge us to tune in tomorrow and tomorrow once again. For many viewers, their characters can take on a reality which exceeds that of the actor who plays the role, occupying a veritable land of make-believe. To act as if part of such a soap opera, as has sometimes been remarked of the behaviour of younger members of the royal family, is no solution, for it is not felt to be the real thing, just condescension.

We too would *like* to believe in the 'happy ever after' syndrome. Of course, who wouldn't! We long for it to be so, as those who went before may also have done, once upon a time. Mario Jacoby (1985) has written of the psychological meaning of a 'longing for paradise', or a wish to be back in a Garden of Eden before the fall. This relates, he suggests, to memories of blissful moments in mother's womb, or at her breast. At those times she was all our world, seeming to promise happiness for ever, with all conflict dissolved. Such longings have an archetypal quality to them, common to all, which recur throughout life at times when such containment is craved for. In truth, it seems, there never was a Golden Age of any shape or form, except in the memory of some and the unfulfilled yearnings of others. Yet such longings possess a psychological reality that is irrefutable, expressed in this instance by the widely held need for Diana to lead a fairy tale life on our behalf. This was true at the time of her marriage: it remained true through her at times unconventional life; and it remains true following her final romance and death.

In some ways, present day culture is more settled than it was when the tellers told their tales. We no longer live in small communities, relatively isolated from our neighbours and often uncertain of survival. Daily tasks like drawing water from wells, cutting and hauling wood for stoves, spinning and sewing in homesteads, are all done elsewhere or by other, less laborious, means. Time lapse and distances have been curtailed or abolished by easy means of transport, while local dialects have given way to widespread common languages. Even the rhythm of light and dark has been taken from us, as electric lamps prolong the day, bringing it into the house itself, to be turned off not by sunset but at the flick of a switch. Reading, writing, and watching have also abolished the need for live story-tellers, whose true time was that of the dark.

Folk tales have become more 'settled' too, since they were written down and turned into literary artifacts, often excised of details likely to offend a more refined audience. This certainly preserves them for ever, but it also deprives them of the possibility of any further evolution, or of relating exactly to the particular situations experienced by those who listened. Instead, all people in all places and at all times will read more or less the same version of any particular story. Its archetypal themes may resonate within us, or leave us cold.

It may seem as if this codification has meant that such tales can no longer adapt themselves to compensate unconsciously for conscious one-sidedness. Yet today's Western society is also unsettled, though in different ways to those of a previous age. Unparalleled mobility between places and classes of people, with voluntary emigration as well as political exile, mass culture, films and television, the Internet, and world-wide fashion trends of every sort, have led to a pluralism of views that is far from any shared vision which might have prevailed in a world that had yet to experience the Enlightenment, that enemy of darkness. In such a situation there is still a pressing need for unconscious revitalisation of conscious fixations. Instead of shared beliefs, there is an unswerving commitment to an over-individualistic pluralism that threatens to make meaningless previous ideas of group commitment and community. In other words there is still a requirement, though different in both aim and content, for the presentation of universal themes whose intention would be to compensate for surface singularities which, in excess, threaten the break-up of society.

So we still need our fairy tales, it seems, to compensate for our one-sided-nesses. Significantly, the director George Lucas had the mythologist Joseph Campbell as a consultant when he made his *Star Wars* trilogy, which is perhaps why those films are so much more satisfying than the as-if-factual *Close Encounters of the Third Kind*, filmed at about the same time.

One inexorable outcome of the Enlightenment view, that progress is certain, has now become, inevitably, one of our greatest one-sided-nesses. Through its development of science and the technology of an indus-trial revolution, First World humanity has become all-powerful, or so it believes, to subvert the courses of natural forces, and to control, for the most part, their basic vagaries. So it has become easy to believe that anything which goes wrong can ultimately be put right through knowledge, that more knowing gives more power. This century has lived within such an unassail-able myth of progress. 'Every day and in every way', it might be said, 'things are getting better and better'. Yet, as a result of this myth, there are no more spirits in the heart of the wood, no central vision to make sense of and give a meaning to human existence. Instead, humanity dares to think itself at the centre of the universe, while science and all its children have taken care of that which was formerly the province of the nether-world we call 'the uncon-scious'. Even the secularised storyteller by the fireside has an electronic voice and eye, undeterred by daylight. Soon, we are told, the very rooms we live in will be able to respond to our whereabouts and moods by means of com-puterised sensors. Even compensation will be electronic.

Because of this partly conscious belief in humanity as master of the fates, we have been led to expect ourselves to be always effective and able to influence and prevail at all levels, whether physical and somatic, or emotional and of the soul. Ultimately then, earthquakes and meteor-strikes, cancers, depressions or road traffic accidents 'should' all be preventable, by human engineering of some sort or another. Happiness 'should' be for ever and any failure for this to come about must be either a 'natural disaster' for which people could never have been to blame, or else, by massive collective projection, the fault of some evil 'other'.

Living at the end of the twentieth century is therefore to exist with a fantasy of possible changes which can only be for the good of humankind. They are, of course, unknown and unknowable because still to come. Yet because of our tendency, or wish, to see the history of this civilisation as a never-ending unfolding towards betterment, optimism carries all before it, blindly surfing the crests of its self-made waves.

Or does it? At the same time, there is a queasy feeling that this may not be so. These are also shadow-times, where old certainties desert, and – as the poet Omar Khayam knew it would – 'the moving finger writes, and having writ, moves on'. The endings of this culture or even human existence may very well be at hand, by means of war, diseases, famine – let alone a planetary despoliation that proceeds unchecked, despite the mouthing of good intentions. As yet, no answers can reveal themselves, except, it appears, an intimation that nothing is for ever – even civilisation. It may be the fact of 'happily for a time' with which, currently, we must learn to live, as well as the destruction of that happiness.

If that is so, then a hint for such difficulties has been provided, I believe, by the choreographer Matthew Bourne and the dance company 'Adventures in Motion Pictures'. Synchronistically perhaps, his reworking of the ballet *Cinderella* was first performed in London during September 1997. The setting is World War II, during the nightly, indiscriminate, aerial bombardment of London by Hitler's air force. At that time, with invasion thought to be imminent, the known world truly did seem possibly to be coming to an end; for many, on the continent of Europe, it already had.

The heroine's father is crippled and in a wheelchair, while the stepmother and her own brood of young men and women are set on having a good time with foreign servicewomen and men – eating, drinking and dancing, for tomorrow they might be dead. Cinderella, excluded from all this jollity, first rescues a wounded British airman who will be her prince to come, then manages, against odds, to attend an invited function at a famous nightclub – all with the help of a shimmering male angel. At the height of festivities, the club is bombed, killing many, and the airman, finding her sequined shoe in the wreckage, fears that she also is dead. But, after a time, they are reunited in her father's house, under the aegis of the angel. From here, the pair must leave, on a train. Whither bound? The suggestion is that it will be the front line again, where the action is.

At that time of European hostilities, of course, there *were* no certainties of any 'happy ever after', but only of the struggle to come, and possible death. And, as Cinderella's train pulls off stage, with happiness in balance, the angel touches another sad young woman on the shoulder, who then dances into life. The never-ending process is set to start again, with different subjects and a different context. For Cinderella and her man the future is uncertain. For how long will they be 'happy' in their togetherness? The question hangs in the air, as it does for the new subject of the angel's attention – and for us all.

For Diana, Princess of Wales, the question had been abruptly answered less than a month before it was posed on stage. Clearly, the facts of her death and the way it happened are tragic. Yet in trying to fathom its meaning to so many people, physical actualities are not so important as their mythic and archetypal resonances. These self-same 'facts' brought out differing emotions in so many people, and in response each one was inescapably disposed to form psychic images which were personal, whatever their universal resonances. That is what Jung meant by an archetypal image, and that is what Diana has become in her death, just as she was, though differently, during life.

This is why her life and death remain so universally compelling; few people seem able to let go of them, even if they deride that public response of which they too are a part. A thousand explanations have been given with, no doubt, a thousand more to come, each and every one 'true' in its uniqueness, as the archetypal imagery of the individual. I have already evoked some of the archetypal themes that arose for myself: the longing for a paradise that is 'happy ever after', and for a world that is certain and fixed in its 'progress' towards that paradise – as well as the knowledge of their opposites. What we reacted to also, and relatedly, I suggest, was the birth of shared hope as well as its so-summary loss.

One who had 'found true love', in a superficial reading at least, had had it snatched away. A week before, many could be cynical about her love, her companion and whether the romance would last. In death, these two became, for ever, 'star-crossed lovers'. One who had triumphed over personal difficulties of many kinds, seeming to be on the edge of a fresh start, was cruelly cheated of her due rewards. Diana, whose charitable work, in the full glare of publicity, could easily remind each among us of various disadvantaged, maimed, or scapegoated parts, was herself snuffed out. A taper was extinguished, candle in the wind, the callous quenching of young life, unfinished but finished off. And yet, her pleas for compassion, all on the verge of being taken seriously, live on.

Hope, and not hope; happiness, but only for a time: the possibilities are all there, presented as if within our grasp at last, and with luck to last. Diana's life and death may serve to remind us that we can experience what we so long for; that we may have that for which we wish; that what we would be, we may be. And yet . . . all is also only for a time, a finite term, before we ourselves return to some universal. Hope exists, hope is destroyed, yet hopes live on.

When Diana was alive, people,whether dedicated watchers of things royal or not, could envy her – for her looks, her style, her money, or her freedom, clothing her with the wildest of their dreams. Now she is dead they can still imagine such things to be possible for themselves – 'for she showed us so', though not, it seems now after her death, for all time. Sharing in that can now become an act of participation with all those others who imagined something similar.

True expressions of genuine emotion are hard, as we British, unused to modes of passionate speech, know well. In such a case, any voicing of emotion may come out mawkish, mushy, maudlin, like the sentiments on cheap greeting cards. The language spoken by the unconscious mind often comes across in this overblown way, requiring conscious refinement. Perhaps the notes and the floral tributes to Diana were the only way in which many who mourned could do so. Struck without warning by a storm of emotion, they blurted out those messages as best as could be, straight from the feeling heart, in its own unconscious, unrefined language.

Many will deride such expression, especially the more intellectually sophisticated, as puerile and cloying. But maybe such cultivated people are those who avoid their own rages of the heart by knowing about them, rather than knowing through embodiment – in symbolic terms, a truly 'carnal' knowledge. Unable freely to emote, believing lust to be only something sexual – rather than simply the joy of and desire for living – the emotionally ill-educated among us (and we are legion, sophisticated or not) should not be blamed for flowery sentiments.

Yet sentimentality is more than just a barrier to clear expression, more than the spontaneous language of the unconscious. Sentimentality also embodies a repressed and therefore unconscious hatred of loved objects. Those who were failed in infancy may hate the parents who failed to mirror back to them the sublimeness of their being, or those who turned away, abandoned, or abused – and rightly so. But for many reasons, conscious or unconscious, it may be neither possible nor politic to speak out, and so rage is disguised by turning it into sentimentality , or a sticky sort of love.

Diana seemed to have all those things that anyone in our acquisitive consumerist age could long for. Power, possessions, beauty, position, money, adulation, as well as a freedom to indulge, all were hers, and in loving her anyone could imagine them as their own, projecting lost parts of themselves upon her. On the one hand, she was loved and admired for who she was and how she behaved as well as for what she represented – especially when seeming to thumb her nose at the dead heart of tradition and authority. (Who would not love to do likewise?) Yet she could also use those trappings to seem more Royal than royal, for which she was certainly envied too. Upon her were projected countless imagined royal selves. 'If only I could be like that . . .', we said.

But as royalty she also became a part of the hated 'establishment' of those in authority, representing parental figures who may once have failed in so many ways. And so a destructive envy also filled and fuelled many hearts and minds. Some openly disdained her as a silly exhibitionist. Others openly admired, all the while secretly and unknowingly loathing her for having and doing all that they would, if they only could. For to own and experience such royalty within the kingdom of the Self – instead of projected into another – may seem to be past all possible imagination. She seemed to have stolen what should be mine, or yours maybe, and we loathed her for it, longing to see some come-uppance, covertly wishing to destroy her. Those who are famed are loved and always hated too, as the tabloid press well knows.

But then she blew it, cast it all away. By dying, she threw it all back in the faces of her admirers, as if their love and admiration mattered not one jot to her. So for that she is secretly hated too. It is as if the unconscious hatred and disdain had killed her just as it wished. And if that affect, just by its existence, was so powerfully destructive, no wonder that it must be tucked away, to be neither acknowledged nor examined. The shame would be too great ever to be admitted. So turn it into adulation.

Diana was also, it was said, manipulative, and of course she could be. She exploited people, settings and situations to suit her own needs – even the very same tabloid newspapers and their *paparazzi*. Her status and position could be used, no doubt about it, to gain what she wished, sometimes intentionally, sometimes unknowingly.

Yet 'manipulative' is a label used and beloved by (usually male) medical personnel and similar professionals to describe a person (often female) with whom they cannot cope, or keep under some version of control. It belittles as it blames. We might recall, however, that this human species has reached evolutionary prominence partly because of such powers. For 'manipulation' literally means to 'handle' (from Latin *manipulus*, a handful), and hands are our premier tools. We also have, as do no other apes, an 'opposing' thumb, one that can move across the palm of the hand. By this means we are able to perform ever more intricate operations of manipulation, giving us an increased power over our environment that has allowed us to use such mastery creatively for good, as well as for evil.

So, symbolically, if not in reality, those who are denigrated as 'manipulative' are only trying, and maybe with some desperation, to handle their lives more creatively. They live in lasting hope of being, at last, in charge of self, and not dispowered. And they never give up, however disastrous the effect of such attempts to control their environment, however often they seem to end up being controlled by others – as was their unconscious expectation, based upon bitter past experience. This is one reason that in her life Diana was loved by so many: she never gave up the struggle despite, reportedly, frequent bouts of despair.

If at times despairing, at others Diana was also branded as hysterical. Hysteria, that age-old and supposedly female disease of the 'wandering womb', first described by Hippocrates, has much the same about it as 'manipulation', though operating through physical symptoms to exert control. Present day psychotherapy has one root in the dramatic performances of female hysterics, under the control of Professor Charcot, at the Salpêtrière Hospital in Paris, where both Freud and Jung studied. By coincidence, it was to that same hospital that the dying Princess of Wales was taken by ambulance.

In our time, the diagnosis of hysteria has always had negative implications, having been used by men to denigrate and manage women, even though it has been admitted since World War I that men can be, and frequently are, hysterics also (see Barker, 1991). Elaine Showalter is currently arguing for such illnesses as Chronic Fatigue Syndrome, Post-Traumatic Stress Disorder and even Gulf War Syndrome to be seen as present day examples of hysteria (Showalter, 1997). Many who suffer from such illnesses are men, but on account of the still adverse implications of such a diagnosis, Showalter has received death threats, despite repeatedly denying any intention of negatively labelling the sufferers.

So it should surprise us little that Diana was seen as hysteric, since this provided a useful label with which she could be denigrated by her detractors – for fighting back against 'Establishment' disapproval, for her changes of heart and her dramatics, and for the eating disorders from which she famously struggled to liberate herself. It has also been scornfully opined that much of the response to Diana's death was 'nothing but hysterical' – a means of labelling which might be a way for the scoffers to gain distance from the very emotions they cannot bear to face within themselves.

But hysteria can be seen as more than just a conversion of psychic symptoms into dramatic and debilitating physical ones, which condemns the sufferer to being labelled with a disease that is 'all in the mind'. Jung understood the conversion of psychic symptoms to be more than a protective psychological defence; like all the psyche's defences, he claimed, this one could also be seen as a way forward, specifically to overcome conscious one-sidedness. He expounded the notion of a 'psychoid realm', neither somatic nor psychic, from which disturbances might be experienced either physically or psychologically (Jung, 1954b). This formulation might release any sufferer, it seems to me, from any shame that 'hysteria' still carries in its train. It also allows us to re-evaluate this age-old disease as a model for flux and change. Nothing need be for ever and Diana's reinvention of herself gave us an example that we too might emulate. Indeed, such a way of being and becoming might now be essential.

In his first published book, *Symbols of Transformation*, Jung laid down a framework for the growth of consciousness that was explicitly based upon hero mythology (Jung, 1912). His pupil Erich Neumann confirmed this theme in his own work *The Origins and History of Consciousness* (Neumann, 1954). Consciousness, according to this view, is a heroic undertaking. Since those days, however, possession of the conscious mind by any single archetype has been defined by James Hillman (1979) as a delusion. Pluralism has become a more powerful flavour of the present age (Samuels, 1989). Polytheistic tendencies present themselves as more relevant and attractive rulers of the human psyche, reminding us that, for the Greeks, to worship only one god was the ultimate hubris (Hillman, 1979). As a corrective, David Miller (1981) puts forward the notion of henotheism – many gods, but only one at a time. Post-modernism denies the relevance of universal 'grand narratives'. In other words, the time of the hero is past. A new model for consciousness should be our aim in which one archetype can rule for a time, to be replaced by another, as required.

Now, no one any longer has to live by the creed of 'once a princess, always a princess' or 'once a hero, forever that same hero'. Instead, 'princess' and 'hero' become one of a number of existences that can be put on, like clothes or when appropriate, changing to suit the mood, the needs, or the demands of time and culture. Now, any woman may be a mother, a saint , a princess, a worker, or a lover – not to mention a slut, a harlot, harpy, wise woman, witch, or bitch. Diana, Princess of Wales, modelled many of those for us, in her time. Her failure to live out only one role – as royal fairy tale princess who lived happily ever after – attracted the accusation of hysteria. Reframing that diagnosis, I would say that hysteria has once again become the illness of our times, but in a positive sense. It can now be seen to point towards a state in which individuals should feel free to endorse and enact their multiple selves.

Human beings have always lived in a changing age, and most likely always will. Humankind is both part of that changing field, and a most powerful author of transformations. At the present time, a settled future seems difficult to predict – or maybe even any future-to-come at all. Central meanings seem irrelevant. A complexity that's hard to fathom becomes our only daily order.

How can we handle this now and in maybe worsening times without lapsing into dumb despair? Charles Handy has suggested the need for the individual to become a 'portmanteau person', carrying a range of skills and willing to adapt to differing circumstances, since no one can really expect to procure a steady job for the whole of life (Handy, 1989). I have myself put forward the model of the master craftsperson with his or her own assembly of mechanisms, each with its differing actions and appropriateness (Tatham, 1992). And that individual toolkit may continue to develop over a lifetime. Jung might have called it individuation.'Well-craftedness', that universal and un-gendered approach to solving problems, transforms them aesthetically by creating, whereas the hero transcends by destruction. Finally, my question 'how can we *handle* this?' returns us to the notion of manipulation, which might now be seen in a more positive light, as the aim of creating order out of chaos, and willingly reentering chaos so as to make further order – like well-craftedness. Hillman refers to our complexes as '. . . labyrinth makers, the artisan craftsmen who cannot cease from shaping' or, following Jung (1921, par. 78) as 'the continual activity of psychic fantasy that makes what we call reality' (Hillman, 1979, p. 119).

Diana's death, her style of living and our reactions to both have modelled for us the ultimate bleakness of all hope, as well as demanding the reaffirmation that the desire for a favourable future can exist within hopelessness. Neither alone is sufficient, for our wish is for survival in both of those two states of being simultaneously: hopelessness and true hope.

To be able to live in doubt without succumbing to despair, or yet to blind optimism, is an achievement. Certainly, each and every person is fated to experience the sorrow of losing all hope, from time to time, as well as the joy of reaching the summits of desire. To survive both hope and hopelessness without denying either is a goal to be striven for.

In our myriad responses to Diana's death – the death of hope – we were, as we are still, drawn together. In our tributes, in the wish that she and her work be not forgotten, in our inability to give up further exploration, we are at one, even though we may disagree as to meaning. Such mutuality of interest, the 'I & thou', exists within the human psyche, as with a mother and her infant, before any individual selfhood crystallises out. In one sense, Diana's death brought about a regression to that prior state. It demanded our participation, taking so many people out of themselves to feel a oneness that is implicit in being human. As a result perhaps people may have been able to share tentatively in some fresh emotional mode that may be transformative of, as well as transcending, present splits and oppositions. Such a modulation would lead not towards a unison of voices, but to mutual enjoyment, with respect for individual difference.

That would be hope. Yet no final state has been achieved, nor can it be. There is no 'happy ever after', for the evil of despair is always waiting to break out again. In a Danish tale, 'The White Dove' (Lang, 1997) the youngest of three princes and his newly-won princess narrowly make it back into the safety of his father's castle, while the witch, in hot pursuit, is turned into a flint stone that sits upon the window sill. Like any flint, that stone could, at any time, spark off another conflagration and the destruction of hope. All is in doubt. The prince and his princess are happy – but only for a while.

REFERENCES

Barker, P. (1991). *Regeneration*. London: Penguin.
Grimm, J. & W. (1975). *The Complete Grimm's Fairy Tales*. London: Routledge & Kegan Paul.
Handy, C. (1989). *The Age of Unreason*. London: Hutchinson.
Hillman, J. (1979). *The Dream and the Underworld*. New York: Harper & Row.
Jacoby, M. (1985). *Longing for Paradise*. Boston: Sigo Press.
Jung, C. G. (1912). *Symbols of Transformation*. *CW* 5. London: Routledge & Kegan Paul, 1956.
— (1921). *Psychological Types*. *CW* 6. London: Routledge & Kegan Paul, 1971.
— (1954a). 'Archetypes and the Collective Unconscious'. *CW* 9 i: 3–41. London: Routledge & Kegan Paul, 1959.
— (1954b). 'On the Nature of the Psyche'. *CW* 8: 159–234. London: Routledge & Kegan Paul, 1960.
Lang, A. (1997). *The Yellow Fairy Tale Book*. New York: Dover.
Miller, D. (1981). *The New Polytheism*, Dallas: Spring Publications.
Neumann, E. (1954). *The Origins and History of Consciousness*. London: Routledge & Kegan Paul.
Samuels, A. (1989). *The Plural Psyche*. London: Routledge & Kegan Paul.
Showalter, E. (1997). *Hystories* . London: Picador.
Tatham, P. H. (1992). *The Makings of Maleness*. London: Karnac and New York, New York University Press.

'My Place in the Crowd': The Princess's People

JOSEPHINE EVETTS-SECKER

Let me first reminisce. In 1952 we were marched into the Junior School hall in enforced silence, sensing something urgent. The headmaster's manner made us quiet. A radio had been brought in and when we were assembled, it was turned on. This was something quite new. A hushed hall heard Big Ben strike, solemn music played and an 'appropriate' voice announced that George VI was dead. The King is dead; long live the Queen. It was a bombshell, though we had no idea why. We filed back to our classrooms subdued, aware that our lives were somehow changed. We caught the significance and were strangely excited by the solemnity.

The next year was dizzying. There was a potent sense of renewal, more renewing for us young girls than the end of the recent war. A Princess was coming to the throne. Since our birth, male voices had dominated the air waves. An hysterical voice (identified as Hitler's) shouted a strange and terrifying language; 'trustworthy' Dimbleby-voices constantly told us things we didn't understand, except through adults' reactions of horror or relief; Churchill's rhetoric had roused even us; and in the midst of it all, reassurance and sanity, our King's measured, rather distant voice had lulled us with an imagined majesty into quiet confidence and national coherence.

The King's funeral passed me by. For me there was no live image, only still icons of ceremonial display and solemn marching music on the radio. Coronation mugs appeared very quickly and everyone rushed out to buy twelve inch Ecko televisions, so that they could 'see' what the people had never seen, the actual crowning of a monarch, a young Queen. Flags and jubilation and a Princess offstage. We did not yet know her voice. Her coronation dwarfed her wedding to the handsome Greek. Ecstatic hype in the papers. Pop songs extolling the Princess-Queen, 'the sweetest queen/ The world's ever seen/Riding through old London town'. We saw the assembling of the Queen of Tonga and all the other international stars, flown in for the great pageant on this little isle. Westminster Abbey was filled with everyone we could dream of. Numberless servants and handmaids of the gods, if not the immortals themselves. Trumpets and Tudor voices and ancient rites; the mysteries unveiled via this new television miracle. The pageant of the century. One of the first real media events.

It was my first experience of television. We were invited to a friend's house to watch for the whole day, eating chicken sandwiches in front of the screen so as not to miss a moment. We were recent eleven plus victors and we giggled with nervous embarrassment when the royal breast of this untouchable Princess was anointed by the Archbishop. What a secret and revered breast that was! We were shocked and excited beyond imagining.

That people's Princess. My childhood memories are impressed with icons of a pretty adolescent dressed in ordinary WVS uniform driving an ambulance, or camouflaged in overalls, tinkering with dirty engines of military vehicles. Our Princess. Like her people, part of the war effort. And then she was transformed: from Bride Princess to crowned Queen. Her youth had gone. She did her duty, dutifully, Athena's own. Her service to the *polis* was practical and staunch.

Then the Reliable Queen began to do what Queens must do: reign solemnly and produce heirs. There was a convenient Queen Mother to play Mother to the Nation while the Queen got on with her own primary preoccupation of a royal and public kind. Then maternal icons of christenings and fledgling princes and princess launched. This poor young Queen had to carry something of the virginal Gloriana of Spenser, a Tudor Faerie Queen, and also bear the image of Victoria, devoted to her Royal Family and her subjects, guiding us into all British virtue, good sense and stability. A decade after the war, people were ready for the new Elizabethan era. She also needed to be a groundbreaking modern, who could cope with the rapidly changing world of the 50's and manage the technological revolution that brought her daily into our living rooms. From the start, her media image was 'managed.' *Public Relations* had entered our vocabulary and consciousness.

That people's Princess became a new kind of people's Queen, sending Princes and Princess to school with at least some of her most loyal subjects. Wherever the Queen went, we followed; every walkabout, every thrusting of flowers into royal hands was broadcast to us. With the wedding of each royal child, a new media series began and with each marriage, our education in soap-opera theory leaped forward. The erosion of royal distance had begun and the nation cheered and grieved simultaneously as we pried. The old order was changing. The fairy tale needed modernization, many insisted. But could the twenty-first century sustain royal fairy-tales; could fairy tales with their kings and queens exist at all in a Britain that might become a republic? Some would claim that the symbolic power of monarchy is all the greater when it is no longer actual, historical reality, when it no longer has actual political power, for then it is more receptive to projection. This questioning of the actual and symbolic power of monarchy fermented in the political psyche throughout this century.

How quickly we seem to have forgotten what has gone before in media discussions of the supposedly 'new phenomenon' of emotional Brits on the streets. Nothing like the Diana-quake had ever happened to the British before. But it was all recognizable too, a different collision of some of the same archetypal energies, though more urgently and critically constellated.

Early in the reign of Elizabeth II, I was a full and largely unconscious participant, like the 'crowds' around me. I too have aged and the glamourous Princess who dominated my early years has become an old woman, struggling to meet the demands of a ticklish democracy in an age of media transparency that has eroded the mystery of royal life. Like the first Elizabeth's and like Queen Victoria's, the Queen's long reign has merged with the nation's sense of its identity and continuity, but there has also been increasing dissatisfaction and disaffection with the royal status quo. Collective hopes were vaguely pinned on Diana for some political and psychological resolution to constitutional crisis, where tensions are growing between monarchy and republic. Diana's style and the new configurations of royalty and democracy that she provoked were certainly making a difference in popular attitudes to such issues. A very human and accessible monarchy, out on the streets and in the midst of the contemporary ills of the people seemed vital and viable, promising a future. Tradition and grace might co-exist with such a modality. Extreme royalist and extreme republican forces have been trying to initiate a twentieth century choice for or against monarchy. Is it possible that Diana represented some form of the transcendent function in the political unconscious of the nation, somehow reconciling these political opposites in a most unexpected way? A creature too multi-faceted and contradictory ever to be one-sided. A glittering and compassionate princess, serious and naive? An absurd enough psychic possibility, to which I will return.

The matured and history-processed Queen will probably die in her bed of old age and be mourned genuinely, in some cases nostalgically. She has been a dutiful and loyal monarch and has fulfilled some ancient archetypal expectations in sombre, traditional ways. Let us also bear in mind that she has been a carrier of new feminine energies. But she seems to have tired of the archetypal pace. It is tempting to see her as an exhausted Demeter, run out of maternal steam, unable either to mother her novice daughter-in-law when she joined The Firm, or to rage and grieve for the lost Princess. Yet nor had she been able, like Demeter herself, to allow the young Persephone her independent vitality; the maiden lurked on the threshold to Hades' underworld, and was carried off by a supposedly shadowy Egyptian playboy. That subterranean consummation produced as many flowers as the arable earth could supply the markets with, every petal a projection. A strange and poignant token of her post-mortem life.

As these mythical cycles were spinning and as we collided with them, the energy produced was such that sociological and historical commentary itself sounded archetypal. Diana's life, and especially her death, established that monarchy cannot be abolished whatever happens to the actual House of Windsor. Americans in the London crowd and many interviewed by satellite, claimed still to mourn their loss of monarchy and they took this Royal Highness as their own. In the realm of psyche, emancipation from royal power seems unlikely. Expired and fictive Kings and Queens still reign, effectively or weakly, however we might argue their titles; Princesses and Princes lie in wait, urgent for union and itching to claim the future. These figures still carry numinous authority, subtly individualized for each dreamer, as no others can, other than mythological or fairy tale projections formed from the same psychic structures and born of the same psychic need.

Diana was a divided, unhappy and bewildered Princess, as well as an ebullient beauty, graceful, opulent and full of vivid, if vulnerable and threatened, life. She could carry global and political substance too, though precariously, and she was learning to harness Logos in its service. The potential of this figure to reign in contemporary fantasy was manifold. In his history of our times, Shakespeare might have made her a minor Cleopatra of the Thames in her infinite variety. Diana was an ascendent female who could flout both the patriarchy and the matriarchal order, fulfilling and negating feminist ideals; lauded as independent woman by some and by others castigated as a Barbie-doll princess. She was a Star, friend of Pavarotti and Elton John, yet a humble aspirant to justice, friend to Mandela and Mother Teresa. In best mythic style, she could doff her tiara and enter the Aids shelter, like Lear naked in a hovel with his fool. She bridged the glittery world of fashion and the seat of Establishment power. She was as much female trickster as goddess: so seen and so mysterious, hiding quixotically behind apparent transparency; unconsciously manipulating concealment and revelation, echoing archaic mystery conventions, as I discuss them elsewhere (Evetts-Secker, 1996). She brought to consciousness, as very public facts, so many of the big issues in contemporary society: eating disorders and disturbance in the relationship to body and mother archetypes; the dysfunctional family; the media crisis with its conflict between privacy and publicity; the atrocities of war, especially for innocent civilian victims; the many problems of marginalized members of society; the ravages of the taboo diseases, leprosy and its contemporary, AIDS.

The icon of her engagement with these two is particuarly vital. Here we watched her touch the archetype of the untouchable and this more than anything else affected her critics and reinforced the admirers in her virtual cult. She was filmed touching leprous bodies, embracing and holding hands with AIDS patients, gleamingly fresh and clean beside the conventionally 'unclean.' She stood her ground with naive strength and confronted the world with a new kind of gracious care, as well as with the capacity to bring reason to bear on irrational and ignorant fear.

The divinely appointed monarch's touch is an ancient rite of healing. One of its native British proponents was James I who defended it in his treatise, *Basilikon Doron* (1599). The reaching out of the monarch to touch and the reaching out of the subject to be touched constitutes a forceful archetypal convergence. Such fantasies lie behind the walkabout, where subjects touch gloved hand of monarch and put flowers into royal hands. Diana pushed this to new limits, removing the glove and touching, flesh on flesh, not just well-washed children thrust in her path, but, like Mother Teresa, the unwashed and the diseased. She reached out from a genuine innocence and naivete, it seemed. 'She touched people', the papers and the commentators kept saying, as did the people in the crowds even more fervently. She touched those she met physically, but more potently, psychically, and her touch came from and reached into unconscious psychic depths. 'I feel numb now' was part of the register of experience at her death and this dynamic facilitated the identification of people with the 'People's Princess'. As analysts, we would do well to heed this manifest hunger for touch. We have banned physical touch from our practice rooms with good conscience, but perhaps with some deprivation of psyche. We are very much concerned with the touching of psyche, its subsequent movement and, perhaps, healing. This collective response is a challenge to our practice.

The other side of all this is equally significant, however. For just as the people created the Princess they needed, and the touch they and the collective psyche craved, so they became 'the Princess's People', those she needed to create, and created to need and needed to touch and heal. To become the Queen of Hearts must be a perilous enterprise, as Alice found in her Wonderland, and this was Diana's declared quest. She was so obviously displaced: her brother claimed the earldom, her husband or sons, the crown. A potent matriarchy currently reigns and a feisty, almost-centenarian Queen Mother holds her own court beyond that. What role was left for Diana, and what kind of power? As so often in such circumstances, woman does what she is supposed to do best: love. A magazine article reported an old woman's experience of Diana when the Princess, in jeans, 'turned up' unexpectedly at a gathering of old folk one Christmas day, supposedly having climbed over Sandringham walls to do so. After this meeting, the old woman suggested, as did many others, that Diana 'had very little love in her life, but she had a lot of love to give'. Through love to power, an ancient strategy; a dynamic inspired by Aphrodite, not Artemis, who would rather hunt. Aphrodite dissolved resistance, even that of Mars, god of war. Yet both Aphrodite and Artemis were in Diana's psychic repertoire. The hunt for love, through love, was on.

Polis and *Eros* and increasingly, *Logos,* came together in a Royal High-ness: a serious concern with certain state issues, an intimate style that valued relatedness and a capacity sometimes to deal thoughtfully and through argument with important social and international issues, in co-operation with world statesmen. Though she was clearly often overwhelmed by them, Diana was strangely able to accommodate all these interests. Think of her more than usually poised and impressive, shortly before her death, pretty even when dressed in military protective body suit, walking the mine-felds of a troubled world. Even here, the melting Aphrodite could appear, with her train of the Graces. And though she was a girlish Persephone, Diana could also play Demeter, the raging mother protecting her sons from public assault by those who wanted to peddle their images.

Britain has been ruled by strong women from Queen Boadicea to Margaret Thatcher; Britannia has ruled through two Elizabeths and Victoria. Diana herself came fully formed from collective needs, aspirations and memories and as the culmination of a process of feminine ascendancy that has been growing significantly since the very masculine second world war, assisted too by the feminist movement. Princess Elizabeth's post-war presence I have already evoked. Her sister married a commoner, a frequent fairy tale motif, sometimes heralding union of ruling consciousness and newly constellating Self. There are numberless princesses who marry woodcutters who have made them laugh or redeemed them from their particular imprisonment. Margaret rebelled, to become a dilettante Princess. Her niece, Anne, represented the people in a novel way, competing internationally as part of the nation's equestrian team. All these developments played with and disturbed the veil between Crown and People that had been carefully woven and kept in place for centuries. But it was already fluttering when Diana began her teasing yet substantial mission. The archetype of hide and seek arises from, and influences, the fundament of our behaviours from infancy to old age. We play with, and are played with by, the mysteries we want revealed but cannot behold. To keep hidden behind the veil and to disclose by shifting it, are both archetypal strategies that can exert tremendous power over the spectator, when manipulated artfully. This archetypal pattern is probably at work in the privacy enigmas so urgent in our present culture. To what extent can those who are willingly 'in the public eye' refuse dis-covery by those whose attentions they seek and need?

When so many archetypes converge, with so many opposites in tension, there is bound to be a huge collective eruption of energy. What history will perhaps record as the Diana-quake was different from earlier royal media events only in intensity, scale and perhaps most importantly, transparency and visibility. It was such an overt eruption, so self-conscious, and yet, enigmatically, so unconscious. The 'Princess's People' were bemused by what was happening to them, but they were utterly clear and articulate about the fact that something was happening, to them and to society. They had been violently robbed of the one who carried both their dreams and their banalities. The eruption of collective grief and loss was voiced as something very personal. To speak only of emotion finally breaking through English stiff upper-lipness was totally inadequate, they knew that. And there was a strange sense of fatedness about the whole set of events, so full of synchronicities and ironies.

In his 'reverie' on the sinking of the Titanic in 1912, Thomas Hardy also felt that sense of an appointment with history which archetypal events often constellate. The ship grew in its dock while the iceberg grew beneath the Atlantic, like betrothed marriage partners awaiting consummation. Then

> . . . the Spinner of the Years
> Said 'Now!' And each one hears,
> And consummation comes, and jars two hemispheares.

Hardy entitled this poem *The Convergence of the Twain,* and it is to this sense of convergence that many responded when the news first came through that Diana had been killed at midnight in a dark underpass.

The crowds had been led to believe that there was some hoped-for happiness brewing for this Princess, perhaps with a foreign play-boy, inheritor of a different empire. Such a union with a non-Christian, foreign commoner would have been a rebellious act indeed. But it could not be; that is how so many felt. There was too much intuition of doom around. The Archbishop who married the Princess on her satin and silk wedding day had invoked the fairy tale's 'happily ever after' ending a little unwisely and with some ignorance in his nuptial sermon, for there are fairy tales that end in absolute destruction and loss; many tales comment on such *lysis* with the final words, 'Yea verily, this is the way of the world'.

A disastrous ending to Diana's story seemed to be accepted as inevitable. But why did this tragic sense pervade so much fantasy? She had everything the modern world offers to keep us secure, not only bodyguards and the world's safest car. Yet everything failed and the collective shock was not a shock of surprise. Why this sense of doom? Did her people need a tragic ending, since the supposed fairy-tale bliss had been aborted? And what constituted that sense of 'Now'?

We know that in every life, every day, hugely powerful projections are shot from one psyche to another. Fallible people carry vastly disproportionate energy and purpose for those around them and when the weight of other people's projections gets too heavy, it may be somatized or acted out in various ways. If we consider what projections Diana carried for 'her people', we see at once how insupportable her burden had become, however much she colluded with it unconsciously.

She was undoubtedly a lightning rod for paradoxical projections. She incarnated majesty and brought it down to the human domain; yet she represented the apotheosis of human ordinariness too. Be extraordinary, her people demanded: reveal to us heights of splendour and glamour and magnificence, overwhelm us with beauty and brightness. But be ordinary as we are; raise us up from our feebleness and the dullness of our dreary lives. Transcend the mundane. Be a humdrum nanny, like Cindrella in her kitchen, caring lovingly for the children of others; but then shimmer and radiate and compel adoration. Be a woman of the world, living dangerously; but be pure and generous, a loving mother fighting for her children, for the world's children. Be saviour of victims and vanquish abuse; but be victim too, like us. Be a thoroughly twentieth century woman, with independent mind and will;

but also be compassionate, re-valuing recently devalued maternal largeness of heart. Be the modern mother too, *sister* to your children; show us the fun of the fair, on a water slide with 'your boys'.

All the faces of Diana in print demonstrate with what willingness and vitality she tried to integrate such paradoxes. But they had surely become impossible to reconcile. An urgent need developed for an Aristotelian *lysis*, a disentangling of a plot that had become too complex. On the concrete level, she could not simply disappear into new nuptial happiness, giving up her public life. If she had defied her public in that way, she would have betrayed it. The Princess was in a no-win situation, as were her people. Diana did not die, she was killed. Of course I reject the conspiracy theories that are now, predictably, appearing. But in some senses, the princess and her people did conspire in her dramatic death, in the classical collusion between hunter and hunted. In many ways, she was publicly sacrificed and her death made conscious many demons and yearnings in the collective psyche. In the end, she was for many an agent of consciousness, though unconscious herself.

I come to my title, 'My place in the crowd . . .' This is a quotation from a young woman, captured by a roving camera, who was asked why she was there, waiting for hours outside Westminster Abbey. She was trying to give expression to an intuition of doom, her own and her Princess's. Her own destiny felt somehow inextricably united with the terrible event and its aftermath. Her tearful comments ended with her insistence, 'I just had to be here, to take my place in the crowd'. That conviction that her place was 'there', one among millions, was emotionally absolute. For many in the crowd, there seemed to be a particular purpose enacting itself; to gain stature not by being exceptional or individual, but just by taking up this allotted place as part of the body of Diana's people, her adherents. For the young woman interviewed, this place in the crowd was her own and it gave her a special identity; she had acted out her role as one of the Princess's People, part of a symbiotic collusion. The old woman who met her that Christmas day claimed, 'Princess Diana had the ability to make you feel you were the only person who mattered'. She raised people from their sense of their own ordinariness. To be one of her Mourners was a significant symbolic identity.

The crowd scenes were both compelling and sometimes quite chilling, confirming some of Jung's fears about collective experience and the psychological condition of the individual once s/he becomes part of a crowd. He suggests that 'when many people gather together to share one common emotion, the total psyche emerging from the group is below the level of the individual psyche' (Jung, 1950, par. 225). Admittedly, there were authentic reports of rare crowd behaviour. But it is not only noise and hysteria that indicate possession by an archetype; intensity, affect and a sense of *numen* are the hallmarks of such energy at work.

At her death, our attention was re-directed from Diana to the dynamics of collective behaviours. Cafe owners left their shops open, with free coffee available to those who were waiting in the streets, while they themselves took up their own places in the crowd. 'I too must be there.' It was sombre festival-time, the world-upside-down, an inversion of the old *topos*. Here the expected disorder was replaced for a week by order; the usual misrule of the crowds gave place to a strangely docile rule. The mobilization of police, in anticipation of serious disturbances, proved unnecessary. It was fascinating to watch and hard to imagine anyone not bothering to do so. It was her People's week and they had to speak for themselves, since no-one proved able to speak for them, despite their pleas; neither monarch nor church could satisfy. It was a platitude shattering time that drove people inwards, even when out on the street. Some mystery had taken hold of the nation and beyond, with a palpable but inchoate sense of spiritual need. The archetype of the divine representative had been activated and now the symbolic carrier had disappeared. The puzzled response of many intelligent observers was strangely like that of Eliot's magi to the birth they had just experienced: 'I should be glad of another death'. For Diana's death seemed to offer possibilities for reflection and perhaps even transformation.

This essay might be written completely differently tomorrow and differently again next week, since there are so many ways of framing this complex happening that took everyone by surprise – politician, historian, psychologist, sociologist, cynic and enthusiast alike. We cannot begin to formulate what really happened, except perhaps by recourse to symbolism. But we can fantasize about what it means for the nation and for each individual psyche. It strikes me that one of the profoundest archetypes constellated in and around Diana was the *puella*, the playful girl. She had perhaps never lived this role in outer life; as a troubled child in a troubled family, she did a fair amount of mothering for her brother, by his account. But here, perhaps, we find the most enigmatic and fruitful archetypal projection that accorded most with her own desire and that of her people. She was required to be sexually exciting and provocative, but to preserve innocence; to be a fertile mother, but to maintain purity; to be, that is, a young, twentieth century virgin-mother. She was required to reform our culture, with that uncanny futurity of the *puella*, but to conserve those values we are in danger of losing as well. Above all else, she was required to stay eternally young, and not age or ossify, as might a dutiful queen.

Puella, like *puer*, can carry vital spiritual energy, which is often misunderstood and misinterpreted, because of its lightness and intense spontaneity. I am reminded of a lovely image of the mythological Diana/Artemis, affectionate daughter of Zeus, imagined by Callimachus:

When Artemis was still just a slip of a goddess, she sat on her father's knee and said:'I want to be a virgin forever, Papa, and I want to have as many names as my brother Phoebos, and please Papa, give me a bow and some arrows, please, not a big set'. . . . With that she stretched out her hands to her father's beard, but hard as she tried, she could not reach his whiskers; and he nodded, laughing and caressing her . . . (Lombard & Rayor, 1988, p. 11).

This image speaks to the yearning Diana carried, both positively and destructively. A slip of a girl in the lap of the great god, she wanted power and purpose and was met by laughter and caress. The anguish of the *puella* is that she can be too quickly dismissed, her energy trivialized. She can be minimized, infantilized and distorted by aspersions of exclusive innocence. Our culture does not know how to love maturing girls; this is an area of deep neurosis. We seem to sentimentalize and/or exploit them. There is much fear of them, because of their power to seduce. Yet we are so susceptible to innocence, longing for it and mistrusting it simultaneously. Zeus, a terrible and yet often playful Patriarch, did caress and cherish this girl-goddess, but he did give her bow and arrows too; he did acknowledge the goddess in the girl. His smile was not patronizing. He allowed her power alongside his own.

Over time, the feminine has been dutiful to parental expectations and domestic ones too. Now it has rebelled, but in doing so has become heavy, earnest and driven by a new set of principles. It feels so victimized and so aroused to reverse that victim role; it seems devoid of gladness and play. Dutiful Princesses have established that they can work, but not that they can play, richly and wholesomely. We might give Diana's story the title 'The Princess who wanted to play'. This does not exclude the possibility of being taken seriously; in fact, it must enforce it, if we can only reform our conception of play.

Ours would seem to be a culture weary of both patriarchy and matriarchy. Is it the *puella* archetype that is currently energising girl-power and related popular phenomena? Its effervescence is much needed in these heavy *fin de siècle* times. Now that Diana is gone, will her people, both men and women, simply look for another *puella* to carry these qualities and functions for them, or will they grasp that vitality and spirit for themselves? The people have elected a *puer* prime minister. So will the Princess's people simply become Tony's people, pinning their disappointed hopes on him, trapping him with their *puer* projections? The opposition leader, another *puer* figure, seems also to represent a rejection of the political patriarch. There seems to be a collective need for revitalization. That need might also be projected onto the Princess's boys, which is perhaps in accord with archetypal necessity. It is possible too that the solemn Prince of Wales himself has been somewhat animated by *puella* energies. In a recent visit to Nepal he demonstrated something of that vital spirit when he mingled informally and shook hands with young girls in a shelter for prostitutes, all of them HIV carriers. This might simply be good PR. But it might also be a genuinely new lightness of touch, indicating a willingness to reach out more innocently to Diana's global crowd.

This, to me, is the chief legacy of Diana to her People: the lightness and leavening she put in the service of political and state life. And she managed this without the levity that contemporary girl-hype so often engages. The *puella* is vivacious and continually evolving, promising the unexpected and the hitherto unimagined. She is also genuinely enigmatic, confronting us with paradox and contradiction. *Multo in parvo*: so little and yet so much.

REFERENCES

Evetts-Secker, J. (1996). ' "Noli" and "Ecce": Dis-covering Psyche'. Lecture No. 254, Guild of Pastoral Psychology Lecture Series. London: Guild of Pastoral Psychology.

Jung, C. G. (1950). 'The Psychology of Rebirth' *CW*, 9. i: 116–34. London: Routledge & Kegan Paul, 1959.

Lombardo, S. and Rayor, D. (1988). *Callimachus: Hymns. Epigrams, Selected fragments*. Baltimore: Johns Hopkins University Press.

About the Contributors

Mary Addenbrooke is an Associate Professional Member of the Society of Analytical Psychology and a member of the Guild of Psychotherapists, with a private practice in West Sussex. She is also a member of the Substance Misuse Services team of the Mid-Sussex NHS Trust and is currently preparing a PhD at Essex University on psychological aspects of recovery from dependence on psychotropic substances. She has published papers on her personal experience of analytic training and the treatment of substance misusers.

Ian Alister is a Member of the Society of Analytical Psychology, in private practice in London and Cambridge, He teaches at the SAP and at the University of Cork. He has co-edited and contributed to *Contemporary Jungian Analysis: Post-Jungian Perspectives from the Society of Analytical Psychology* (1998), and is Review Editor of the *Journal of Analytical Psychology*. He has also written a social history of Barnsley Football Club in the 1950s. He is especially interested in the significance of popular culture in clinical material, both as a form of language and as a range of contemporary myths.

Michael Anderton is a Senior Analyst of the Independent Group of Analytical Psychologists and an Anglican priest. After taking a degree in economics, history and medicine at Cambridge, he became a schoolmaster and subsequently trained for the ministry at Westcott House, Cambridge. He served in the London Diocese before going to Zurich with his wife Robin and daughter Sophia to train at the C. G. Jung Institute. He now works as a priest and analyst in London. He is a Fellow of the Guild of Pastoral Psychology and a founder member of the Guild of Analytical Psychology and Spirituality.

Ann Casement is a Training Analyst of the Association of Jungian Analysts and other training bodies, and Chairman of the UK Council for Psychotherapy. She is a Fellow of the Royal Anthropological Institute and a member of the National Association for the Advancement of Psychoanalysis in the USA. She contributes regularly to *The Economist* and other journals, and is an Assistant Editor on the *Journal of Analytical Psychology*. She is the editor of *Post-Jungians Today: Key Papers in Analytical psychology* (1998).

Warren Colman is a Professional Member of the Society of Analytical Psychology, in private practice in St Albans. He graduated in English and Sociology from

Keele University, failed to become a rock guitarist and took up social work with drug addicts, qualifying as a social worker at the London School of Economics. He trained in counselling at the Westminster Pastoral Foundation and as a marital psychotherapist at the Institute of Marital Studies (now Tavistock Marital Studies Institute), where he was a staff member from 1982 until 1997. He has published numerous papers, mainly on sexuality and couple relationships.

DAMIEN DOORLEY is a Training Analyst of the Association of Jungian Analysts and on the Editorial Board of *Harvest: Journal for Jungian Studies*. He was born in Galway and grew up in Yorkshire and Cornwall. Before training as an analyst he was a teacher, in England and abroad. He now has a private practice in London and teaches on a number of UK training courses.

JOSEPHINE EVETTS-SECKER is a member of the Independent Group of Analytical Psychologists, with a private practice in Whitby. Born and brought up in England, she has recently retired from the English Department of the University of Calgary in Alberta, where she taught for 30 years. She has published many articles on renaissance subjects and literature and psychology, as well as poetry. Her collections of fairy tales for children (Barefoot Books, 1996, 1997, 1998) have been translated into several languages. She is a regular lecturer at the C. G. Jung Institute in Zurich, where she trained.

JIM FITZGERALD is a member of the Independent Group of Analytical Psychologists, in private practice in London. He studied classics at Cork university, going on to research in Byzantine Greek at the University of London. After a period in university administration, he became a primary school teacher. He later studied at the Central School of Speech and Drama in London and trained at the C. G. Jung Institute in Zurich. He has been Visiting Lecturer on the Sesame postgraduate course in Drama and Movement in Therapy at the Central School, and Chairman of the C. G. Jung Analytical Psychology Club, London.

ELIZABETH GORDON is a member of the Independent Group of Analytical Psychologists, with whom she trained. She read history at Cambridge, worked for Amnesty International and then lived abroad with her diplomat husband. She now has a private practice in London and is currently Chairman of the C. G. Jung Analytical Psychology Club. Her interest in the Amazon archetype, which has not yet let her go, arose out of a thesis written during her training. Other interests include life-drawing and sculpture, obsessional gardening and writing. She is married, with two sons.

JANE HAYNES is a Professional Member of the Society for Analytical Psychology, a member of the Site for Contemporary Psychoanalysis, and the Review Editor of *Harvest: Journal for Jungian Studies*. She trained as an actress, and started her career at the Royal Court Theatre in the early 1960s. After reading *The Divided Self* by R. D. Laing, she decided to give up the theatre and work with him, and she helped him organize *The Dialectics of Liberation* at the Round House, London in 1967. She now has a private practice in London. She is co-editor of *The Place of Dialogue in the Analytic Setting: The Selected Papers of Louis Zinkin* (1998).

JULIET MILLER is a member of the Association of Jungian Analysts and of the Institute of Psychotherapy and Counselling. After studying at the University of Kent, she joined the BBC to train as a film editor. For many years she worked as a freelance documentary film producer for the BBC and Channel Four, and her films on women's, environmental, political and development issues took her to Africa, India, the Americas and Europe. She now works in London, in private practice and for the Westminster Pastoral Foundation.

RENOS K. PAPADOPOULOS PhD is Professor of Analytical Psychology at the University of Essex, training and supervising analyst of the Independent Group of Analytical Psychologists and Consultant Clinical Psychologist at the Tavistock Clinic in London. He has co-edited (with Graham S. Saayman) *Jung in Modern Perspective* (1984),edited the four-volume *C. G. Jung: Critical Assessments* (1992), and co-edited (with John Byng-Hall) *Multiple Voices: Narrative in Systemic Family Psychotherapy* (1997). He has been working in various countries as consultant to international organisations, such as the UN and the Council of Europe, with regard to psychological consequences of violence and disaster.

ANDREW SAMUELS is Professor of Analytical Psychology at the University of Essex and a Training Analyst of the Society of Analytical Psychology. He is a Scientific Associate of the American Academy of Psychoanalysis and a member of the executive committee of the International Association for Analytical Psychology. He also works as a political consultant. His publications include *Jung and the Post-Jungians* (1985), *A Critical Dictionary of Jungian Analysis* (with Bani Shorter and Fred Plaut, 1986), The *Plural Psyche* (1989), *The Political Psyche* (1994) and *The Secret Life of Politics* (forthcoming). He also edited *The Father: Contemporary Jungian Perspectives* (1986) and *Psychopathology: Contemporary Jungian Perspectives* (1989).

ANN SHEARER is a Senior Analyst of the Independent Group of Analytical Psychologists, with which she trained and of which she is currently Convenor. After reading history at Cambridge, she worked for twenty years as a journalist, for *The Guardian* and freelance. Lecturing and consultancy in aspects of social welfare also took her for many years to different countries across four continents. She now has a private practice in London and teaches for several psychotherapy training organisations. Her books include *Disability: Whose Handicap?* (1981), *Building Community* (1986), *Woman: Her Changing Image* (1987) and *Athene: Image and Energy* (1996, 1998).

PETER TATHAM is a Senior Analyst of the Independent Group of Analytical Psychologists, and a member of the Severnside Institute for Psychotherapy in Bristol. He qualified as a doctor in 1959 and spent ten years as a general practitioner before going to Zurich to train at the C. G. Jung Institute. With his wife, who is also a psychotherapist, he now lives and works in Devon. He lectures and teaches in both England and Scandanavia, and has published a number of articles on Jungian themes as well as *The Makings of Maleness* (1992). He is currently engaged with a book on 'fathering'. He has four daughters and two granddaughters.

Index

Pavarotti, Luciano 155
Penthesilea 96, 97, 99
'People's Princess' 3, 54, 156
Persephone 94, 155, 157
persona 60–3
Philip, Prince 83
Pisces, age of 22
Pitié Salpêtrière Hospital 2, 148
Polis/Eros/Logos 75, 76, 155, 157
politics and psychotherapy 37–45
Presley, Elvis 72
Press Complaints Commission 119
primal scene 40–2
Prince of Wales *see* Charles, Prince of Wales
Private Eye 126
psychotherapy and politics 37–45
Puer/Puella personality 32–3, 93, 161–3

Queen *see* Elizabeth II
Queen Mother 94, 153, 157

Redfearn, J. W. T. 135
religious aspects 91–2, 110–12
Renault, Mary 100
Rilke, Rainer Maria 94–5
ritual 50
Rorschach, Hermann 12
Roth, Philip 104
Royal Family
    collective self-worth and 52–3
    criticism of 4, 30, 54, 109
    Diana's exclusion from 18, 92
    struggles of 106, 125–6, 155
Royal Standard 3, 4–5
Rumens, Carol 81
Runcie, Robert 19
Rushdie, Salman 25
Russian culture/icons 67–8

sacred, nature of 51–2
St James's Palace 3
saintliness 24, 110
Salpêtrière Hospital 2, 148
Self (Jungian) 40, 52, 87
self-injury 63, 66
sentimentality 146
sexuality 24
    maternal sexuality 44
shadow archetype 48–9, 66, 92
Shand Kydd, Frances 34, 125
Showalter, Elaine 148
Shrine, The (TV documentary) 36
Simpson, Wallis 125

Singer, A. 118
Smith, Joan 115
Snowdon, Earl of 126
Spencer, Earl (Charles) 34, 116, 124–5
    funeral oration 3, 6, 56, 71–2, 78
spirituality (virtual) 69–72
Star Wars trilogy 143
stars (celebrities) 58–60
    collective dimension 63–7
    star to icon 67–9
stranger archetype 25
Sun, The 106
symbols 46–7, 112
Symbols of Transformation (Jung, 1912) 149

Tarkovsky, Andrey 118–19
Tavener, John 67, 77, 78
television 83
    Forest of Bliss 118
    Modern Times 113–14
    Panorama interview 10, 13, 66–7, 97
    The Shrine 36
Teresa, Mother 82, 155
Teresa, Saint 24
Thatcher, Margaret 40, 110
Times, The 7
touch, healing 34, 35–6, 156
    royal healers 50, 156
Townsend, Peter 126
Townsend, Sue 28
trickster archetype 48–9
    trickster-anima 110
Turner, Victor 47
TV *see* television

Vanity Fair interview 25
Victoria, Queen 85
Virgin Mary 15, 82, 92, 110–11
Virgo, sign of 94
virtual reality (VR) 71
virtual spirituality 69–72

Westminster Abbey 124
    see also funeral of Diana
William, Prince 4, 5, 15, 53
Windsor Castle 83
Winnicott, D. W. 103–4, 120
Women's movement 76, 97
wounded healer 32, 34–5, 127, 134

Yeats, W. B. 89

Zeitgeist 42–3